Dance-Punk

Forthcoming in the series:

Dance-Punk

Larissa Wodtke

BLOOMSBURY ACADEMIC
NEW YORK • LONDON • OXFORD • NEW DELHI • SYDNEY

BLOOMSBURY ACADEMIC
Bloomsbury Publishing Inc
1385 Broadway, New York, NY 10018, USA
50 Bedford Square, London, WC1B 3DP, UK
29 Earlsfort Terrace, Dublin 2, Ireland

BLOOMSBURY, BLOOMSBURY ACADEMIC and the Diana logo are
trademarks of Bloomsbury Publishing Plc

First published in the United States of America 2021

Bloomsbury Publishing Inc does not have any control over, or
responsibility for, any third-party websites referred to or in this book.
All internet addresses given in this book were correct at the time of
going to press. The author and publisher regret any inconvenience
caused if addresses have changed or sites have ceased to exist, but
can accept no responsibility for any such changes.

Whilst every effort has been made to locate copyright holders, the
publishers would be grateful to hear from any person(s) not here
acknowledged.

A catalog record for this book is available from the Library of Congress.

ISBN: PB: 978-1-5013-8186-7
        ePDF: 978-1-5013-8188-1
        eBook: 978-1-5013-8187-4

Series: Genre: A 33 1/3 Series

Typeset by Integra Software Services Pvt. Ltd.
Printed and bound in Great Britain

To find out more about our authors and books visit www.bloomsbury.
com and sign up for our newsletters.

Contents

Prologue—That's How It Starts

Turning eighteen at the turn of the millennium in Winnipeg, the geographical center of Canada, I found myself simultaneously shaped by the post-punk vanguard of the 1970s and 1980s and the post-punk revival occurring in real-time. While I do not want to dwell on my personal relationship with dance-punk, especially since I did not live in the urban centers in which these scenes flourished, I do think my lived experience and memories shape the way I understand the genre.

For me, the latter half of the 1990s, in which I spent high school, was dominated by ubiquitous boy-band/girl-band pop of the Max Martin variety, post-grunge alt rock that sounded so alike that "alternative" lost all meaning, the unholy blend of heavy metal and hip-hop that was nu-metal, and the ADHD arrested development of pop-punk. There was both a strangely elated hype leading up to 2000 and a sense of creative exhaustion. Unlike some of my peers, I did not have Internet access at home, so my music world was relatively confined to the influence of friends, Top 40 radio, and the Canadian version of MTV, MuchMusic.

The only music that made it through my teens and into young adulthood was David Bowie, Prince, New Order, and a handful of 1980s new wave compilations; the rest was jettisoned as I began to discover sounds beyond my relatively sheltered sphere. My most voracious absorption of music occurred between ages eighteen and twenty-eight, a time of revival and recovery in the form of garage-rock throwbacks like The Strokes, The Hives, The Libertines, and The White Stripes, the goth reimaginings of My Chemical Romance and Fall Out Boy, the return of New Romanticism through the fantasy of electroclash, and, of course, the moment when punk kids began to dance again.

Initially, my tastes expanded through books and magazines, which only increased once I took a part-time job at a bookstore during university. The bookstore provided access to imported music magazines, books on the histories of popular music genres, and album reissues. It also became the trading site for many burned CDs between my coworker Jay and me that ranged from LCD Soundsystem and The Rapture, to Kitsuné Maison compilations, to Phoenix and Saint Etienne, to Modular Records bands like Cut Copy, The Presets, and Van She.

Between 2000 and 2007 I began to travel regularly to the UK, mostly with a friend whose father worked as a pilot for British holiday flights in the spring and summer. Living, and sometimes working, in places ranging from Stockton-on-Tees to Ashby-de-la-Zouch to Cardiff, my newfound access to music not readily available in my part of Canada only strengthened the Anglophilic tendency in my tastes.

By the mid-2000s, with increased access to high-speed Internet, the popularity of MySpace, and the advent of MP3 blogs and their aggregators, I could keep up with the most popular new songs circulating at the time while learning about older, rarer music in specific genres and geographies. An MP3 blogger myself, I actively entered into this community, eventually writing my master's thesis on it. As others who experienced the 2000s as a formative period can attest, I experienced popular music as a continuum where different historical periods, geographies, and styles could be immediately contextualized. At once I discovered and listened to Joy Division and Interpol, Orange Juice and Franz Ferdinand, The Clash and Mcclusky, the Velvet Underground and the Jesus and Mary Chain, my father's Kate Bush records and my own Patrick Wolf CDs, Soft Cell's "Tainted Love" next to the Gloria Jones original, Camera Obscura's "Lloyd, I'm Ready to Be Heartbroken" alongside Lloyd Cole and the Commotions' "Are You Ready to Be Heartbroken?"

I found dance-punk at the same time that I was making my way through the back catalogs of punk, post-punk, indie, and dance music. It may be a quirk of my Asperger's brain, but I am greatly intrigued by creating and tracing idiosyncratic genealogies and patterns of culture. I love both Greil Marcus's *Lipstick Traces* and John Higgs's book on the weird magical mythologies and coincidences surrounding the KLF; I'm also an enormous fan of the exploded theories in stark Helvetica in the documentaries of Adam Curtis (friend of dance-punk originators Gang of Four), as well as artist Amy Siegel's 2016 video meditation, aptly entitled *Genealogies*, on ideas of remaking and copying through the lines between Freud, paintings of de Chirico, the Villa Malaparte, and Jean-Luc Godard's *Le Mépris (Contempt)*. And I was exactly the type of retromaniac described in Simon Reynolds's 2011 book, *Retromania*, enjoying the pastiche and intertextual play of television series like *The Mighty Boosh* and *Flight of Conchords*.

My relationship with cool and its sister concept hip is also bound up in music, especially the music of this period. Music acted as a catalyst, identity marker, and world maker as I tried to forge some sense of self. Becoming an expert on certain types of music made me feel a Bourdieu-like distinction and belonging.

I ended up loving music that made me think, but also music that made me dance, and if a song could do both, even better. I had and still have no claim to being cool or hip, but I was keenly aware of the parallel rise of the hipster during the first decade of the twenty-first century, and its close association with, among other scenes, dance-punk. If I'm being honest, I participated in quite a few facets of hipsterdom. I still do enjoy many of the things associated with hipsters: skinny jeans, heavy-framed glasses, "artisanal" comestibles, a desire to be part of the so-called "creative class," obscure bands, Wes Anderson films, books like *A Heartbreaking Work of Staggering Genius*, *High Fidelity*, and *Kafka on the Shore*, and a finely honed sense of irony. I probably still care more than I should about how my tastes are seen by others.

Over time, I've become more critical about how I've been shaped by a culture that is unevenly dictated by middle-class, white males. I'm none of these things. I grew up in a working-class family—albeit one that had middle-class sensibilities and tastes—and was the first of my family to attend university. Growing up, I felt no connection to my Chinese grandfather who passed away when I was three and whose t(race) remained on my own face. I'm female, but don't feel a particular allegiance to or identification with gender. I've come to realize how much my intersectionality matters, but my liminality, my in-betweenness, has complicated my relationship with dance-punk. I remain a fan, but perhaps a more critical one.

Part of dance-punk's magic is how it takes two sides of a supposed mind-body split and reunites them. Some would argue that the transcendent quality of dance music cannot and should not be reconciled with intellectualizing and rationalizing. Like many of the artists I write about, I can get far too obsessed with details and criticism, rather than just feeling and understanding through that feeling. With this book I hope to convey the excitement and movement of dance-punk while sharing my sense of pleasure in thinking and theorizing through it. But sometimes you have to stop making sense.

1 Genealogies and Constellations

When you search *dance-punk* using the website *Every Noise at Once*, the "algorithmically-generated, readability-adjusted scatter-plot of the musical genre-space, based on data tracked and analyzed for 5,173 genre-shaped distinctions by Spotify," you end up with a cumulus word "cloud" composed of over a hundred different musical artists. The Milky Way-like core of the chart is perhaps expected, featuring the names that have most come to represent dance-punk, such as LCD Soundsystem, Death From Above 1979, and Le Tigre. Near the misty edges you will find English post-punks This Heat, American neo-gothic revivalists She Wants Revenge, German-Norwegian indie-pop band The Whitest Boy Alive, Steve Albini's post-hardcore rock outfit Shellac, and DFA synth-poppers Holy Ghost!

In this visual representation, temporality is obliterated, and spatial relations are made strange as Gang of Four abuts Franz Ferdinand, which, in turn, nestles under Peter, Bjorn, and John. In another cluster, Magazine, Broken Social Scene, Mclusky, and Arcade Fire hover in close proximity. To fans of these bands, it may appear jarring or even incorrect, but if you pull back and regard the whole, it tells a story of dance-punk as a genre and posits interesting questions about what gets included and what does not.

Moving away from quantitative machine-learning, the Apple Music playlist "Burn the Dancefloor: A Raucous

History of Dance-Punk," compiled by journalist and author Liam Inscoe-Jones to accompany his article by the same name,[1] reveals a similarly disparate range of artists and bands, including additional names like Sparks, The Stooges, Joy Division, the B-52's, Foals, and Hot Chip, but still core commonalities like LCD Soundsystem, Death From Above 1979, and Le Tigre. As both machines and humans end up with comparable constellations rather than stable, linear genealogies, the complexities and uncertainties of genre definition are evident, but so too are the traces of a repeated canon.

This fuzzy lack of clarity amid persistent areas of agreement is repeated in the handful of other dance-punk compilations and lists found on the Internet. In a recent guide posted within the celebrity-as-teacher learning platform MasterClass, dance-punk is defined as a "rhythmic blend of dance floor grooves and punk aggression in the '70s and 2000s" exemplified by LCD Soundsystem, Hot Hot Heat, The Pop Group, The Rapture, and Test Icicles.[2] They argue that the three main characteristics of the genre are related to the instrumentation, lyrics, and vocals. Most crucially, the rhythm section is placed in the foreground, alongside aggressive guitars, to give traditional punk a danceable groove. Dance-punk lyrics provide a wider emotional range ("confrontational," "edgy," "introspective") than dance music lyrics, which they read as largely about "emotional release." Meanwhile, intense, rather than melodic, vocals lend the dance music beats a punk edge.

These characteristics are so vague and subjective that they could be applied to any number of genres. To say simply that dance-punk is a hybrid of dance and punk is both deceptive and reductive. So, what are we really talking about?

Defining Dance-Punk

Dance-punk, like many compound musical genres, does not exist in a standard dictionary. In *Appetite for Definition*, Ian King's "A to Z Guide to Rock Genres," he admits that dance-punk could be "open enough to allow in danceable punk rock from any era," but acknowledges that "when people refer to dance punk, they are typically speaking about one of two particular periods: the post-punk bands who began dabbling in disco-like rhythms at the end of the 1970s, and the cluster of bands who sprung up in the early 2000s and clearly admired the former."[3]

According to King, there are several crossovers between dance-punk and genres such as art punk and new wave, and I would argue there are several more, including no wave, mutant disco, and electronic rock. Within the *Every Noise at Once* dance-punk scatterplot alone, electroclash, alternative dance, new rave, neo-synthpop, and indietronica are listed as overlapping sub-genres. Alternative labels for dance-punk, including disco-punk and punk-funk, also reveal that there are additional sites of crossover. These hybrids tend to grow out of two primary roots: disco, the 1970s dance music invented by people of color and LGBTQ+ people, and its late '60s predecessor, funk, as defined by Godfather of Soul James Brown and his "rhythm on the one" (related to both a cosmic Black unity and the emphasis given to the first beat of each measure). These roots are then grafted onto the other major musical subculture of the '70s, punk rock.

The interchangeability of these terms mirrors the complexity of the dance-punk genre. One common thread might be that these artists borrow from a wider spectrum of styles that are only cohesive in that they are seen as different from, and perhaps in opposition to, punk. Arguably, disco became the more ambiguous genre of "dance" as it headed back underground after its mainstream implosion and literal destruction at the infamous Disco Demolition Night in 1979. As disco morphed into genres such as house, techno, rave, trance, and garage, the descriptor "dance" became diluted to those without insider knowledge of the myriad micro-genres within it.

Notably, the punk attribution in the dance-punk/disco-punk/punk-funk group remains the same, implying that all music in these genres retains an essence of aggressive, guitar-based music that rebels against and operates outside of the mainstream, rooted in late-twentieth-century nihilism toward economic recessions and the hypocrisy in society, politics, and popular music itself. Of course, the spectrum within the genre of punk is broad, ranging from more melodic early bands like Sex Pistols, the Ramones, and The Clash to the speedier hardcore of Black Flag, Dead Kennedys, and Minor Threat. This range finds its way into dance-punk, marking the difference between the sound of Death From Above Records (better known as DFA) and Death From Above 1979.

Given its permeable, imperfect nature, it's fair to question the point of analyzing a genre like dance-punk. While it's important to remember that genres are rarely of interest to the artists themselves—and are often unwanted labels—they are essential tools of taxonomy for fans and critics, which help us tell stories and make sense of an otherwise random world. As music scholar Mimi Haddon observed in her study of post-punk, genre is indicative of how certain types of popular music come to represent specific values and disavow others to maintain structures of taste and ideology, forming canons that very often reflect the subjective position of white, Western heteropatriarchy.

Dance-punk, which originally emerged in the wake of late '70s disco and punk, demonstrates these reflections of genre. It also inherits the ambiguity of its root genre post-punk, whose tree of limbs includes the industrial noise of Throbbing Gristle and Cabaret Voltaire, the synthesizer soundscapes of The Human League and Simple Minds, the ska sounds of 2 Tone, the uncompromising nihilism of no wave, and the playful indie pop of Postcard Records.

Over the last two decades post-punk has been historicized and theorized by several authors, including Simon Reynolds, Mimi Haddon, and David Wilkinson, all of whom cover some of those who would be classified as dance-punk artists (Public Image Ltd., Gang of Four, James White and the Blacks, etc.). In Reynolds's seminal book, *Rip It Up and Start Again*, the first to attempt to describe the post-punk genre, he makes the argument that unlike punk, which was nihilistic and creatively restricted to the point of becoming a cultural cul-de-sac, post-punk was forward-looking, inventive, and productive.

As Haddon notes in her 2020 book, *What Is Post-Punk?*, Reynolds's view of post-punk is that it is a "quasimodernist genre motivated by experimentation and an inclination toward the new" and "driven by radicalism and stylistic eclecticism."[4] This contention of Reynolds that post-punk is valuable and good because it is progressive and new deeply influences his later book, *Retromania*, in which he argues that the popular culture of the early twenty-first century is obsessed with its recent past and is therefore unoriginal and uninspiring, specifically noting the early 2000s post-punk revival as a symptom of this failure.

The aesthetic of modernism comes up again in *Are We Not New Wave?*, Theo Cateforis's book on post-punk's more commercial sister genre, new wave, which like post-punk includes some dance-punk under its umbrella. Cateforis maintains that new wave was indicative of a modernist impulse with its display of a nervous aesthetic, its use of irony and kitsch, and its colonial appropriation of non-Western cultures. Despite these modernist tendencies, the fact that both post-punk and new wave drew from popular music rooted in punk shifts them into what philosophy scholar Bernard Gendron terms "borderline aesthetics," in which the avant-garde and popular commingle. In other words, these genres position themselves as both *against* the avant-garde practices of genres like progressive rock, and *as part of* an avant-garde that focuses on new and futuristic styles. In a sense, then, post-punk and new wave already contain stylistic contradictions that are then passed on to dance-punk, which has its own unresolved paradoxes.

At the crux of dance-punk is the apparent tension between the resilience and emotion of dance music and the cynicism and irony associated with post-punk and indie rock, with all of the racial, gendered, sexual, and class connotations that are implied. There are further frictions between what is considered authentic, original, or cool, and what is pretentious, derivative, or uncool.

The Socioeconomic Context

Behind these value-laden judgments lies the backdrop of late capitalism and its accompanying ideology of neoliberalism, both of which frame the emergence of dance-punk in the 1970s and its resurgence in the 2000s, shaping the literal and figurative landscapes of the genre.

My use of the term "late capitalism" here relies on literary critic Fredric Jameson's *Postmodernism, or, the Cultural Logic of Late Capitalism*, in which capitalism from the 1970s onward is defined by multinational corporations, ever-accelerating computerized automation and planned obsolescence, ever-growing mediatization of people's lives (where television, film, publishing, and the Internet reinforce capitalism through everyday culture), and the totality of American military and economic domination in the wake of Soviet communism's demise.

Often used interchangeably or alongside late capitalism, neoliberalism is an economic ideology that mandates market deregulation under the guise of individual freedom. Under neoliberalism, government protections are reserved for private property, corporations, and those in the highest wealth brackets, while state-provided services such as healthcare, education, and housing are diminished. As David Harvey and others have noted, neoliberalism has come to permeate all facets of life, effectively becoming the underlying belief system. Individuals are solely responsible for their own wellbeing, which is mostly measured in financial terms, and they must endlessly compete with others to achieve success. A large part of this competition is ensuring that you're resilient, or capable of bouncing back after trauma or a crisis, especially as people cope with "the uncertainty and instability of contemporary capitalism as well as the insecurity of the national security state."[5] Surviving and thriving is each individual's responsibility, obscuring the socioeconomic systems that impact the ability to achieve happiness.

The Intellectual and Aesthetic Context

The late 1970s and early 1980s, in which dance-punk first emerged, is also the period when the aesthetic theories of postmodernism and poststructuralism both advanced to question the assumptions, grand narratives, and ideologies of the modern. With its origins in the eighteenth century, modernism sees science and reason as the basis for a universal truth and inevitable human progress. According to modernism, our selves are stable and coherent, and language is transparent in that it always means what it says. By contrast, postmodernism suggests that there is no universal truth, asserting that everything is subjective and relative. In short, modernism believes in a concrete, objective reality while postmodernism sees all reality, including one's own identity, as constructed and compromised by culture, language, and personal experiences. Similarly, poststructuralism questions cultural and societal structures, including language, demonstrating that all interpretations and experiences are biased and fluid rather than stable.

Modernism and postmodernism are further complicated by their associations with particular artistic movements, the former located in the late nineteenth and early twentieth centuries, the latter associated with the mid- to late twentieth century. Modernism was characterized by experimentalism and a break with realism in both literature and visual art, producing novels like James Joyce's *Ulysses* and paintings like Picasso's *Les Demoiselles d'Avignon*. Modernism had utopian and future-fetishizing impulses, which generated a proliferation of manifestos and -isms, including Futurism, Vorticism, Suprematism, Cubism, Surrealism, and Constructivism. Modernist art was often ironic, but the irony was rooted in a sense of liberation, striving toward some sort of unity and order despite the apparent fragmentation of the world. It is this kind of modernism that Reynolds, and to some extent Cateforis, sees in the post-punk and new wave music of the late 1970s and early 1980s.

Postmodernism, which can be seen as both an intensification *of* modernism and as a paradigm shift *after* modernism, is defined by a rejection of logic, a liberal borrowing of past styles in the form of pastiche, the dissolution of high and low art, and an irony that did not seek to unify but rather accept the crisis of representation. Pop Art, like that of Andy Warhol, Conceptual Art, as in performance pieces by Carolee Schneemann and Yoko Ono, and work by the Young British Artists, including Damien Hirst's tiger shark suspended in a tank and Tracey Emin's messy bed, are all postmodern. In its 1980s heyday, even MTV was considered postmodern in its blurring of programming and advertising. In Fredric Jameson's view, postmodernism also signaled a "waning of affect," which can be interpreted in both senses of *affect*: the postmodern subject "becomes emotionally numb, or at least strikes a pose of indifference, and senses an inability to cause change or comprehend cause and effect."[6] Postmodern irony is used not as a self-reflexive move to create critical distance but to admit that there can be no critical position.

Admittedly, these tangents into cultural and socioeconomic theory may not seem immediately relevant to the world of dance-punk, but these larger contexts are deeply reflected in the genre. For example, New York City, one of the key locations of dance-punk in both of its major incarnations, is pointed to as an early harbinger of what neoliberalism would be in practice. After essentially going bankrupt in 1975, the city slashed public services and municipal sectors that had been the product of strong working-class labor movements. A year later, the United Kingdom, another crucial location for first-wave dance-punk, fell into the same circumstances with the collapse of the pound forcing the Labour government to request a loan from the International Monetary Fund in exchange for implementing austerity measures in a way that parallels New York.

Dance-Punk as a Compromised Genre

The first wave of dance-punk emerges in the midst of these system shocks by attempting to create a communal, alternative scene to critique the growing push toward neoliberal competition and private accumulation. This scene not only formed the vanguard of art and music, but of the hipster colonizers who settled urban spaces that once housed the working class and people of color. The second wave of dance-punk would come together in an urban world dominated by the figure of the hipster who worked in creative industries, trafficking in the symbolic rather than the manufactured and hoarding subcultural capital.

I see dance-punk as both modern and postmodern. In descriptions of dance-punk, which often include adjectives such as *angular*, *dry*, and *minimal*, there is an aspiration to be rationally modern in order to be more valuable as art, rather than merely repetitive dance music for entertainment. Like its parent genre post-punk, dance-punk can be seen as drawing on modernist tropes, aural approximations of the minimal geometry of El Lissitzky, Kazimir Malevich, and Wyndham Lewis. At the same time, postmodern irony and flatness dominate the dance-punk genre, exhorting the listener to dance without compensatory or celebratory narratives of resilience and overcoming. Less "I Will Survive" and "Promised Land," more "Contort Yourself" and "Get Innocuous!"

Perhaps this lack of affect and sincerity is a comment on the impossibility of fighting for a more socially just system, or maybe it's because the majority of the artists making dance-punk were and are from relatively privileged backgrounds, and therefore have no stake in resilience or truly changing the status quo. Also, the resilience espoused in dance music had become a tool of neoliberalism to produce never-ending, unsustainable demands on people, especially the most marginalized. Nevertheless, an overall disenchantment with the rigidity and apparent uselessness of punk and indie rock pushed dance-punk onto the disco floor.

As music scholar Charles Kronengold asserts about new wave as a genre, dance-punk is interesting precisely because it is "compromised or mixed," forcing it to "respond to competing values and practices."[7] By virtue of its hybridity, dance-punk is located at the nexus of what became indie rock and club culture throughout the 1980s and 1990s. Wendy Fonarow's comparison chart of dance versus indie in her book *Empire of Dirt: The Aesthetics and Rituals of British Indie Music* is illustrative here. Dance is assigned adjectives such as *synthetic*, *extroverted*, *for body*, *mindless*, *empty*, *pleasure*, *hedonistic*, and *future-oriented*, in opposition to indie's characterization as *organic*, *introverted*, *for mind*, *intelligent*, *substantive*, *pathos*, *austere*, and *past-oriented*.[8]

Interestingly, Fonarow's chart bears a resemblance to the comparison of classical music with rock and pop in musicologist John J. Scheinbaum's book *Good Music: What It Is and Who Gets to Decide*. Here, classical music is assigned qualities such as *mind* (intellectual), *complicated*, *innovative*, and *genius*, while rock/pop is categorized as *body* (sexual), *simple/common*, *derivative*, and *craftsperson*.[9] The similarities speak to the way these value systems can shift in order to claim the superiority of genres over others, whether between classical and rock, rock and pop, or indie and dance. In all of these comparisons, the mind and intellect are viewed as superior to the body and feeling.

Throughout his book, Scheinbaum discusses the core values associated with "good" music, namely, *seriousness*, *unity*, *depth*, *authenticity*, *the heroic*, and *originality*. The goodness here implies both a moral judgement and an artistic one. Scheinbaum ultimately concludes that these values can interact and work with their opposites (i.e., music that embraces seriousness and fun at the same time). By shifting back and forth between opposing values, musicians can break music out of narrow parameters and make it more interesting. In fact, he sees the breakdown of the border between mind and body as a more fulfilling way to experience music, writing: "The traditional binary opposition between body and mind is no longer aesthetically—let alone scientifically—tenable. Indeed, it's the conjunction between body and mind, the entire person working as a unit, wherein our ability to explore music deeply lies."[10]

About This Book

I am not a musicologist and will consequently not analyze dance-punk from a highly technical, structuralist point of view. Instead, I am interested in the ideas that circulate through popular music and the associations and meanings that are ascribed to cultural texts at various points in time.

This book is not an exhaustive survey of every band that has or may be classified as dance-punk; the scope would be too large and redundant. Instead, I focus on the artists that represent the vanguard of both the late 1970s (Talking Heads, James White and the Blacks, Bush Tetras, Liquid Liquid, ESG, A Certain Ratio, Gang of Four, Delta 5, Au Pairs) and early 2000s (!!!, The Rapture, Radio 4, Liars, LCD Soundsystem, Franz Ferdinand, Bloc Party, Death From Above 1979) more so than the artists who trailed in their wake. Some bands only had a few songs that could be heard as exemplars of the dance-punk genre, such as Public Image Ltd. ("Death Disco," "Fodderstompf," "Memories") and Joy Division ("Transmission," "She's Lost Control"). Some bands, like Liars, only made one album (*They Threw Us All in a Trench and Stuck a Monument on Top*) that could be considered dance-punk. There are yet other artists whom I considered but ultimately discarded for being too experimentally funky/jazzy (The Pop Group, 23 Skidoo, Konk, Medium Medium), too punky (The Slits), and too generally indie rock (Yeah Yeah Yeahs, The Futureheads, Maxïmo Park, The Rakes). It's impossible to make a firm distinction and/or define solid borders for a genre that, according to the discourse that defines it, can range from stronger electronic influences to post-hardcore leanings.

As noted by Mimi Haddon in the case of post-punk, the genres of both first-wave post-punk and dance-punk were named and curated decades after they first emerged. Therefore, much of the dance-punk genre was conceptualized retroactively, and as with the post-punk revival of which it was a part, dance-punk was circumscribed by those who participated in and promoted the second wave.

In the next two chapters I will provide an overview of the times and spaces in which dance-punk originated and operated: the first wave that happened circa 1978 to 1984, primarily in New York City and postindustrial cities of the UK, and the second wave that occurred roughly between 1999 and 2007, again in New York and the UK. Part of this context is briefly tracing the histories and features of two of the genres from which dance-punk emerged: disco and punk.

The fourth chapter focuses on what I see as the characteristics that define the style of dance-punk, including the use of space and minimalism, groove and syncopation, angular guitars, dry acoustics, flat vocal style, and ironic lyrics. The fifth chapter explores the relationship between dance-punk and "the Other," with its racialized, gendered, and class-based orientations and political implications. I end with thoughts on where dance-punk currently stands as a genre, especially as we are now potentially seeing a second revival.

Ultimately, the story of dance-punk, or at least the story I am going to tell, is one of artists negotiating the anxieties and imperatives of living under neoliberalism and reacting to the mind-body split implied within musical styles. As with many genres, the periods in which dance-punk emerges and flourishes are relatively brief, and the bands who begin them change, move on, break up, and occasionally come back. A hybrid, dance-punk destabilizes other popular music genres and exposes how pluralistic and contradictory they actually are. From the Mudd Club to Plant Bar, the dance floors of the Haçienda to Optimo Espacio, dance-punk made mythology and history by mining failure and ugly feelings for transcendent disco diamonds.

2 Death Down on the Disco Floor: The First Wave of Dance-Punk

Emerging as it does from disco and punk, dance-punk is strongly associated with urban space, especially as it is mythologized and idealized. These spaces—imagined and real—evoke atmospheres of cosmopolitanism, artistic freedom, and rebellion against the parochial mainstream.

In particular, pre-1980s New York City is held up as an artistic maelstrom, attracting people escaping the narrow-mindedness of their hometowns. At the same time, in the 1970s—one of its most lauded creative periods—New York was, in reality, a post-apocalyptic place, ravaged by socioeconomic wars. Amid a national period of stagflation, the bankrupt city did not appear to have a hope of recovering as the more affluent white population fled to the suburbs. It was a city in crisis, rotting and burning in the throes of late capitalism. For a glimpse of this world, one need only watch *Downtown '81*, the surreal film starring artist Jean-Michel Basquiat alongside his contemporaries Arto Lindsay, James Chance, Fab Five Freddy, and Debbie Harry.

Nevertheless, the artists featured in *Downtown '81* are a significant part of the persistently romantic image of New York as a haven of coolness and creativity. During the 1970s, New York and its extensive network of clubs became an incubator for musical innovation, first with disco and punk, and then with its fusion, dance-punk, which coexisted and sometimes collaborated with the nascent hip-hop scene brewing in the Bronx. Rents were low so artists could afford to devote most, if not all, of their time to pursuing their creative interests amidst the ruins, but they were living on borrowed time as city officials began to explore ways of luring corporate interests to the city with tax breaks and subsidies.

The rosy view of this period sometimes obscures the fact that the scene was also partially bankrolled by privileged individuals with financial capital like Michael Zilkha, owner of ZE Records, Rudolf Piper, co-founder of Danceteria, and Steve Mass, owner of the Mudd Club. Notably, while the artists emerging from New York itself were largely non-white, the majority of the artists who were attracted to New York from other cities were white, presaging the rise of gentrification, more slowly in the 1970s and 1980s and then exponentially in the 1990s and 2000s. Gentrification homogenized the city and its boroughs as it scrubbed away the signs of danger and difference. Many have studied and lamented this shift in New York, including books by Sharon Zukin (*Naked City: The Death and Life of Authentic Urban Places*) and Jeremiah Moss (*Vanishing New York: How a Great City Lost Its Soul*) and documentaries like Kelly Anderson's *My Brooklyn* and Marc Levin's *Class Divide*. This move to gentrification is at the heart of the dance-punk story with its first and second waves bracketing the emergence of what author Samuel Stein calls "the real estate state."

Undergoing a similar trajectory, gentrification in the UK often appears in the guise of regeneration and uses popular music histories to promote nostalgia tourism, as is the case with the legendary status of Factory Records and its music scene in Manchester. The 1970s in Britain saw a massive rise in unemployment, especially in cities that had been deindustrialized, marked by numerous strikes, power cuts, and the three-day work week. However, unlike the neoliberal times to follow, wealth inequality was actually at a record low and many musicians were still able to attend art school through grants, art schools being a part of the country's post-war consensus. As in New York, the bleak environment inspired musicians to first rebel and rebuke through punk, and then to merge the punk aesthetic with the hedonistic freedom of dance. The disappointment and frustration largely remained but was transmuted into a dance amongst the absurdity.

Therefore, dance-punk first appeared at the point of dislocation, a Rubicon of sorts for the socioeconomic order. As the United States and the United Kingdom began the move toward Ronald Reagan, Margaret Thatcher, and their policies of economic deregulation and privatization, musicians responded with a mix of critique and bodily pleasure. As we will see later, dance-punk reappears at the turn of the millennium after the so-called "end of history," when the triumph of capitalism collapses in the debris of the World Trade Center. By that point, neoliberalism had seemingly become the only reality, and dance-punk, in thrall to the mythologies of past urban imaginaries, reveled in its own impotence.

Dance, Dance, Dance: 1970s Disco

In his history of disco, *Turn the Beat Around*, Peter Shapiro traces its origins all the way back to the affluent youth subcultures of the Second World War, including Germany's Swing Jugend and France's Zazous, who defied Nazism by dancing to hot jazz played by disc jockeys. Postwar, this type of underground dance culture shifted to what the French called discothèques, which included Whiskey à Gogo and Chèz Régine in Paris and the Peppermint Lounge, El Morocco, and Arthur in New York. At the same time, Black clubs in Harlem, Brooklyn, and Manhattan were hybrids of gatherings commonly found in African American communities—rent parties and "jooks"—that produced "atmospheres that were halfway between a bar and someone's house."[1] While clubs like Arthur predicted the "body fascism" of later disco clubs like Studio 54, these Black clubs are prescient of David Mancuso's Loft, which brought together a diverse group of people to dance to the all-encompassing sound system in his home in the 1970s and 1980s.[2] Meanwhile, in the wake of the Stonewall riots and the birth of the gay liberation movement, dance clubs like The Sanctuary opened and catered to a gay audience, which would come to define disco as a sexually ambiguous and hedonistic genre.

According to Tim Lawrence's history of dance music culture in the 1970s, the music played at clubs like The Loft and The Sanctuary was eclectic and not yet a genre. Songs included Manu Dibango's "Soul Makossa," Curtis Mayfield's "Move On Up," James Brown's "Get Up I Feel Like Being a Sex Machine (Parts 1 and 2),"The Temptations'"Law of the Land,"The Beatles' "Here Comes the Sun," and The Marketts'"Out of Limits." It is also during this period that the disc jockey, or DJ, becomes a mixer, attempting to blend songs into one relatively seamless flow. Early disco was heterogeneous due to limited mixing technologies, with a preference for records that maintained what is now called a "four to the floor" beat and a tempo of 120 beats per minute. Songs also tended to feature extended instrumental sections for easier blending.[3]

Peter Shapiro credits The Sanctuary DJ Francis Grasso as a major influence on what would become disco's sound. Grasso's choices made disco distinctive from soul and funk by favoring records with a less aggressive rhythm and an atmosphere of alienation, such as Little Sister's "You're the One," a record produced by Sly Stone and featuring his sister Vanetta. In noting how some of Grasso's selections had a darker feel that departed from the positivity of the hippy 1960s, it is interesting that Shapiro uses words like "alienation" and "deracinated," which imply that the rooted blackness connoted by the more "aggressive" funk, which often celebrated Black pride and unity, is becoming undone in the shift toward a disco sound.[4]

In her book *Hot Stuff: Disco and the Remaking of American Culture*, Alice Echols corroborates this aspect of disco's formation. She writes of the way disco opened up Black masculinity, which had been typically represented by the aggressive "sex machine" image of funk, to more feminine, romantic configurations, while moving gay men from stereotypical effeminacy toward a macho style most visible in a band like The Village People.[5]

Echols observes that it is difficult to "map a genealogy of disco" in comparison to the "more ostensibly 'underground' punk" even though disco borrowed liberally from myriad popular sources.[6] Some of these borrowings included a modification of the pounding beat of Motown Records, as heard on Eddie Kendricks's 1972 track "Girl You Need a Change of Mind." Produced by Frank Wilson, this song was different from the typical Motown output due to two innovations by Wilson: an "inversion of Motown's four-on-the-top beat and his deployment of the gospel break, which emptied the track of most instrumentation and then gradually built it back up."[7] Wilson's technique became a staple of 1970s dance music, eventually referred to as the "disco break."[8]

Rather than the typical heartbeat basslines, four-four snare, and tambourine of Motown percussion, disco concentrated the four-four on the bass drum accompanied by different patterns on the cymbals.[9] Disco also borrowed from funk but differed in terms of texture. According to Echols, the "angular funk" of James Brown, including "his tense, staccato funk, with its unpredictable breaks and bridges … has a ruptural quality different from the plush, tightly seamed, 4/4 steamroller of disco."[10] This textural difference is worth noting since dance-punk often tries to mix both approaches to rhythm.

Another major influence on disco was Philadelphia International Records, founded by songwriting and production duo Kenneth Gamble and Leon Huff. Echols describes the Philadelphia sound as working "the highest end, the sweetest registers of soul music" with its "brassy and up," rather than "down and dirty," feel.[11] The house band for Philadelphia International, MFSB (short for Mother, Father, Sister, Brother), is frequently credited with "turning the beat around" to invent the disco beat in songs like Harold Melvin and the Blue Notes'"The Love I Lost."[12] This lightness and lushness gave disco a sense of sophistication and opulence, which was often critiqued as shallow and materialistic.

Throughout her book, Echols also troubles the easy narratives and binaries of disco, demonstrating that assumptions about Black and gay subcultures cannot be confined to defeat and accommodation, in the case of the former, and liberal leftist inclusivity, in the case of the latter. Discussing the experience of African Americans in the 1970s, she describes the decade as a time of "heightened sense of possibility."[13] Rather than bemoaning the failures and regressions that followed the promise of the 1960s civil rights movement, as well as the economic stagflation of the day, she writes that "[f]or black musicians, claiming the mantle of sophistication was a thrilling proposition, even if the end result sounded like schmaltz and looked like a sellout to some."[14] Like the excesses of subsequent hip-hop, disco functioned as an expression of aspiration, and for Black people, who had often been relegated to the lowest socioeconomic classes, it makes sense that they would want to attain a better standard of living, even if it were, in the words of the Ashford & Simpson song, "Bourgie Bourgie."

A prominent example of this aesthetic and attitude is the music of Chic, cofounded by Nile Rodgers and Bernard Edwards after years of playing in funk, lounge-jazz, and R&B outfits. Band biographer Darryl Easlea notes Chic stood out from other disco artists because their music is a "very blank, repetitive sound."[15] Echols points out that Chic also fostered a "tony style drawn from the look and posture that Bryan Ferry and David Bowie put forward during their 'decadent' period."[16] She credits Rodgers for thinking: "If we take this sophistication, high-fashion, aristocratic, interesting, cerebral stuff, put a beat to it, make it black and our own thing, we could really be happening, too."[17] In so doing, Chic appealed to buppies (or "Black yuppies"), but also those who would create dance-punk. Along with another dance-punk favorite, Donna Summer's Giorgio Moroder-produced "I Feel Love," Chic shares characteristics with music by white Europeans—in Summer's case, Kraftwerk's "Trans-Europe Express"—which represents the nuanced side of disco and foreshadows the hybridity and ambiguity of dance-punk.

Just as materialism was embraced by Black disco fans, Echols argues that "it took gay liberationists a decade to acknowledge the obvious—that gay men were about as likely as the working class to renounce the pleasures of consumption and sign onto a socialist revolution."[18] In his essay, "In Defence of Disco," film scholar Richard Dyer acknowledges that this tendency toward materialism can be difficult to defend from a socialist or feminist perspective, concluding, "Disco's combination of romanticism and materialism effectively tell us—let's us experience—that we live in a world of materiality, that we can enjoy materiality but that the experience of materiality is not necessarily what the everyday assures us it is."[19] In exploring the potential of the romanticism in disco, Dyer sees disco as providing a "flight from [the] banality" of everyday sexism and racism, which can then be interpreted as an escape from capitalism and patriarchy.[20]

As such, disco is often understood as the "territory of the Other."[21] In Echols's view, funk was more male-centric while disco was female-centric,[22] displaying a contrast between the staccato thrust of funk and the fluid cyclicity of disco. She writes, "the very sound of disco was, in contrast to most European-derived music, sonically open-ended (or 'anti-teleological') and therefore anti-phallic," and it "was the music of 'jouissance'— blissful pleasure."[23] Dyer agrees with this anti-phallic rhythmic aesthetic but argues that disco "restores eroticism to the whole of the body, and for both sexes" through its playful polyrhythms and range of percussion.[24]

Despite these aspects that pushed against heteropatriarchy, disco and its sub-scenes were not always as accepting as they appeared. The gay macho clone style popular in many clubs reinstated a normalized way to be masculine or a man, excluding more effeminate gay men as well as transgender people. Furthermore, disco clubs could be intersectionally discriminatory, with The Saint banning women, the Tenth Floor primarily for white gay men, and Paradise Garage arranging segregated nights for white and Black audiences. Echols also points out that disco often reinforced stereotypes of Black women's sexual looseness, as well as promoting whitewashed or "bleached" R&B, offering Donna Summer's "frosty vocal" style as "another depressing piece of corroborating evidence."[25]

In looking at disco with this kind of intersectional lens, recognizing the overlaps and gaps between sexuality, race, and gender, disco shows that advancement in one aspect of identity could simultaneously be regression for another group.

As commercial interests caught on, disco became the answer to the recession in the record industry, making up 40 percent of all chart activity at its peak.[26] But with this boom came an inevitable loss of quality control, with the music industry doing what it often does when it sees a profitable trend: greedily seizing upon it and flooding the market with substandard versions of the genre. These issues exacerbated the belief that was already circulating about disco's inauthenticity. Critics of disco argued that it "had reduced the dance beat to its most mechanical basics" and that "[a]nyone could dance to disco because it was so simple and predictable—it pandered to the lowest common denominator and lacked a genuine groove."[27]

The oft-cited height of disco hitting the mainstream, the 1977 film *Saturday Night Fever* and its multi-platinum-selling soundtrack, whitewashed and heteronormalized the genre, but this popularity only hastened disco's demise. Echols remarks on the move to the right that precipitated this downfall: "By the midseventies a sizable number of onetime liberals, dubbed neoconservatives, were joining with longtime conservatives to mobilize 'Middle America' against abortion rights, affirmative action, school busing, sex education, the Equal Rights Amendment, welfare, and 'criminal-coddling' civil liberties."[28] At this time disco became the scapegoat for permissiveness, partly because "a music that was tailored so precisely to the sensibilities of sexual and racial minorities was always going to repel or embarrass some listeners in the wider society, as the irony and sexual ambiguity of disco were far less capable of translation to the mainstream than the music."[29]

The symbolic end of disco is almost always located at Comiskey Park in Chicago on July 12, 1979, when radio personality Steve Dahl created Disco Demolition Night to promote a doubleheader between the Chicago White Sox and the Detroit Tigers. Baseball fans received a discounted admission fee for turning in disco records, which were blown up at midfield with explosives to the chants of "Disco sucks!" The backlash and discrimination were not only part of the mainstream, though, as disco became a whipping boy for another 1970s music genre.

Who Put the Bomp: 1970s Punk

In the inaugural issue of *Punk* magazine in 1975, disco was excoriated as the "epitome of all that is wrong with western civilization," with editor John Holstrom rallying against its "rootedness in the studio and repetition."[30] In *The Village Voice*, Marc Jacobson observed how the editorial and writing staff at *Punk* "consciously rejected the whole notion of the hipster as 'white negro' and dedicated themselves to celebrating all things teenage, suburban, and Caucasian."[31]

Not only was punk anti-hip but it was also anti-art, laying bare a conflict between authenticity and pretension that can be traced to punk's earlier roots. As Bernard Gendron explains in his book *Between Montmartre and the Mudd Club: Popular Music and the Avant-Garde*, the idea of punk music was essentially invented by American music writers Lester Bangs, Dave Marsh, and Greg Shaw in reaction to what they saw as "arty" and "pretentious" music of the early 1970s, a disparate group that included artists such as James Taylor, Led Zeppelin, and Elton John. According to Gendron, "[t]hey introduced the label 'punk' into the rock discursive stream to identify what they thought to be the paradigms of 'real' or 'authentic' rock 'n' roll."[32]

This discourse began in 1970 when Greg Shaw founded the fanzine *Who Put the Bomp*, which championed garage rock from the 1960s such as Count Five, ? (or Question Mark) and the Mysterians, the Seeds, and the Troggs as the authentic antidote to the slick, pompous rock of the early 1970s. Around the same time, Lester Bangs, writer for Detroit-based *Creem*, contributed to the formation of punk discourse by promoting three themes: "sheer aggressiveness and loudness," minimalism, and "defiant rank amateurism."[33] In Gendron's view, these last two aspects "began a theme that was to become a mantra of the 1970s alternative discourses, which is that rock 'n' roll is at its best when 'stripped down' to its 'bare essentials'—an antidote to the increasing complexity and pretentious experimentalism besetting the music."[34] Eventually, these proto-punk garage rockers would be canonized in Lenny Kaye's 1972 compilation *Nuggets: Original Artyfacts from the First Psychedelic Era, 1965–1968*.

At the same time, Gendron outlines what he calls "borderline aesthetics" at work within punk. This style, "which presents itself as an anti-art aesthetic, functions also as a strongly pro-art aesthetic."[35] Gendron elaborates:

> Being against art simply meant being against the unmediated appropriation of mainstream art notions and their pretensions into popular music—the pieties of the singer-songwriters, the virtuosic convolutions of some heavy metal, and the classical music quotationalism of British art rock. Yet at the same time, the punk aesthetic was clearly incorporating avant-garde notions that came from outside the rock 'n' roll ambit.[36]

This same artistic lineage is exposed through Greil Marcus's *Lipstick Traces*, which connects punk to earlier avant-gardes like Dadaism and the Situationist International, the latter movement particularly inspiring punk svengali Malcolm McLaren with its critique of capitalism's mediation of social relations through what they called the "spectacle." In other words, punk was referencing the "right" kinds of art, much as later post-punk artists would reference the "right" kind of Black music, namely, dub instead of blues.

In addition to their belated valorization of garage rock artists, the early proponents of punk also began to incorporate the "canonizing discourses on the Velvet Underground tradition."[37] These features, which eventually found their way into punk, include not only "two- to three-chord minimalism" and "aggression toward the audience," which were ostensibly already part of the garage rock sound, but also "self-conscious aestheticism and purposeful shock tactics, as well as the dashes of irony" that exist in contrast to garage rock's "stripped-down musicianship," which was "hardly a matter of intention and … not the result of a thought-through aesthetic."[38] With the addition of this discourse, a sense of deliberate provocation and detachment is introduced to the chaotic, authentic style of punk.

Alongside this rock critic discourse, an actual nascent punk scene began to develop, first at the Mercer Arts Center, with bands like the New York Dolls and Suicide, and then at CBGB, which became the stage for punk bands like the Ramones, Richard Hell and the Voidoids, and the Dead Boys, as well as bands that hovered around the artier edges of punk such as Blondie, Television, the Patti Smith Band, and Talking Heads. Not only were Talking Heads not punk but they were, according to Bernard Gendron, "the best dance band at CBGB's and the only one whose rhythms were rooted in African American music."[39] This style is in deep contrast to American punk bands who, "[b]y aligning themselves with the strict duple subdivisions, driving rhythms, and diatonic melodies of early 1960s surf and garage bands, … placed themselves within what was perceived as white musical lineage."[40] Talking Heads' latent tendency toward rhythm is, of course, borne out with their move toward a dance-punk sound as the 1970s turned into the 1980s.

The British punk scene, with its short and chaotic rise and fall documented by Jon Savage in *England's Dreaming*, differed from the American scene in lyrical content and its embrace of Black dub-reggae. Unlike their American punk inspirations, whose politics were "internal to the music" (or pitting alternative music against the mainstream), British punks often focused their lyrics on "the welfare system, capitalism [and] consumer culture."[41]

Furthermore, as Gendron notes, British punk "sported a jadedness, a world-weariness, an all-knowingness, that was barely enunciated in the more innocent aggressiveness" of American punk.[42] That said, this jaded attitude is absolutely to be found in the proto-punk of the Velvet Underground. The mixing of the British punk scene with the West Indies immigrant milieu of Britain may not have always manifested in as obvious ways as The Clash's cover of "Police and Thieves," but this Black influence did indeed have a massive impact on the post-punk bands that rose from punk's ashes.

Not only was punk representative of "borderline aesthetics" but it embodied multiple related paradoxes: "it hymned authenticity but relied heavily on simulation in its performance; it aspired to success on its own terms but glamorized failure; its do-it-yourself aspect raised the issue of how to take and keep control in a genre that glorified the individual against the corporate machine; and it presented itself as a simple negation and as something far more knowing."[43] In the end, these tensions pulled first-wave punk apart, with one of the most notorious examples being the role Malcolm McLaren played in his Situationist experiment managing the Sex Pistols, provoking for provocation's sake and deliberately placing the band in untenable "situations" for the sake of art, prompting Johnny Rotten to utter the now famous line at the Sex Pistols' last gig at San Francisco's Winterland Ballroom: "Ever get the feeling you've been cheated?"

But these unresolved dialectics that make punk interesting as a genre did not extend to the musical style, which relied on an "even quaver static bass line (which was already familiar from early heavy metal)."[44] In fact, "far from being revolutionary," according to music scholars Allan Moore and Remy Martin, punk rock "merely crystallised many of the undercurrents already present in the playing of some rock bands," specifically the anti-virtuosity and taboo subjects of the Velvet Underground, the image construction and three-minute singles of David Bowie, and pub rock, "which had re-established a place for uncomplicated music in small venues."[45]

Ironically, punk bore similarities to disco in how it was seen as derivative, simplistic, taboo, and potentially ironic. The primary difference lay in what may be called their function and relationship to embodiment—that is, how the music is felt and how it affects the movement of the listener's body. While disco's function was to enable endless dancing and a prolonged sense of ecstasy, punk's function was to release frustration and boredom in quick bursts of expediency. As Dave Laing notes in his book *One Chord Wonders*, the anti-syncopated high speed of punk songs conveyed urgency because "if the pace of a song no longer functions as an impetus to dance it then becomes a sign that the singer needs to get across the message as quickly as possible."[46]

By the time both disco and punk hit their explosive ends—the former at Comiskey Park, the latter at Winterland Ballroom—musicians on both sides were looking for a way out of the straitjackets their respective genres had become.

A Quick Pit Stop on the Autobahn: Krautrock's Influence on Dance-Punk

In the late 1960s and early 1970s, young West Germans were searching for a new sound that would reject the British and American popular music that came to dominate the country as much as British and American air bases following the Second World War. They also positioned themselves against their parents' legacy of Nazism and the insipid Schlager music that allowed them to escape thinking about this legacy. Bending the newly invented synthesizer to their whims, artists like Faust, Cluster, Kraftwerk, Can, and Neu! turned to electronic music and experimental composer Karlheinz Stockhausen to forge a new German identity and break from the loaded past.

This new music would be dubbed Krautrock in the British music press—though often called Kosmische (translation: cosmic) in their home country—and ultimately created a genre that seceded from the blues origins of rock 'n' roll in an effort to stay more authentically German. Alternatively, like disco, it reveled in repetition, non-phallic structure, collectivity, and the child-like Id. At the same time, Krautrock was, in the words of music journalist David Stubbs, "travelling but 'going' nowhere at once," in a stasis that "hints at an underlying Sisyphean futility."[47] And in the case of a band like Kraftwerk, who branded themselves as robotic "music workers," repetition did not express a loss of self in sexuality or ecstasy; instead, its flow was serene through order and precision. Julian Cope, singer for Liverpudlian post-punks The Teardrop Explodes, describes Krautrock as "what Punk would have been if Johnny Rotten alone had been in charge."[48]

By 1977, the year that punk and disco peaked, Krautrock had mostly ended. Nevertheless, it left a deep impression on dance and punk music alike, pushing out like a cybernetic web through David Bowie's *Low* and *"Heroes"* to post-punk, dance-punk, and the electronic dance music of the future.

This Heaven Gives Me Migraine: The 1970s Post-Punk Turn

In his history of the post-punk era, *Rip It Up and Start Again*, Simon Reynolds argues that post-punk was a flowering of innovation between 1978 and 1984 that "saw the systematic ransacking of twentieth-century modernist art and literature."[49] Considering dance-punk is essentially a subgenre of wide-ranging post-punk, Reynolds's book unsurprisingly includes many artists who either dabbled in or came to represent dance-punk—which he usually refers to as agit-funk, avant-funk, or mutant disco—including Public Image Ltd., Gang of Four, Delta 5, Au Pairs, Bush Tetras, James White and the Blacks, ESG, Liquid Liquid, and Talking Heads.

More specifically, in her book on post-punk as a genre, Mimi Haddon pinpoints the emergence of post-punk to the "New Musick" issues of *Sounds* in late 1977, which described this new music as "the white equivalent of dub," combining "darkness, melodrama, bookish intellectualism and political leanings, some loosely artistic or avant-garde practices, and, with the Gang of Four in particular, an emergent relation to the mainstream in the form of disco."[50] Haddon acknowledges that the distinction between punk, new wave, and the new musick were not clear at the time and retrospectively coalesced through gatekeepers and tastemakers. Over time new wave came to include some post-punk artists but also others who are not.

In *Are We Not New Wave?*, Theo Cateforis categorizes new wave as a popular music embraced by a music industry that deemed punk too confrontational for mainstream America.[51] He includes bands such as Talking Heads, Blondie, Devo, Adam and the Ants, Gary Numan, and The Knack, "all of whom shared punk's energy but tempered its vitriol with more accessible and novel songwriting sprinkled with liberal doses of humor, irreverence, and irony."[52] At some point, the casual definition of new wave expanded "to encompass nearly any new white artist whose music employed synthesizers or sounded particularly good on the dance floor"[53] and subsequently became known as "electropop, synthpop, and technopop."[54]

Cateforis describes the reorientation of new wave in relation to its predecessors, disco and punk: "'Four to the floor' bass drum hits, open hi-hat accents, syncopated bass riffs, and stratified textures: all these elements suggest a strong link between disco and new wave's orientation as studio-based dance music. Just as importantly, new wave's aesthetic alliance with disco also signified the music's growing distance from its punk roots."[55]

First-wave dance-punk borrows laterally from contemporary genres such as disco, funk, dub-reggae, and Krautrock because they are external or perhaps foreign to punk in order to be read as progressive and new. As noted earlier, punk was not based on a groove, especially as it tended toward a fast tempo more suited to the vertical, isolated, relatively stationary movement of pogoing than the horizontal, relational, sinuous dancing associated with disco, funk, and reggae. At the same time, dance-punk often retained elements of punk or art rock, which ensured that it would still be considered new rather than a retread of existing genres.

Public Image Ltd.

The band that appears in several definitions of dance-punk is Public Image Ltd. (commonly abbreviated to PiL), the group John Lydon (Johnny Rotten) originally formed with guitarist Keith Levene and bassist Jah Wobble after the breakup of the Sex Pistols in 1978. While PiL are second only to The Fall for their infamous revolving door cast, the songs most associated with dance-punk occurred during the original, and what many see as the classic, lineup.

To me, most of PiL's first two albums, *Public Image* and *Metal Box*—though absolutely indebted to dub-reggae in terms of the swirling, oneiric spatiality, echo effects, and melodic bass—are not particularly dance-punk. That said, "Fodderstompf," the final cut on *Public Image*, demonstrates a shift to a dance-punk direction as it foreshadows the "studio-as-instrument methodology of disco and dub" that PiL would use on *Metal Box*.[56]

Its lyrics reveal that this song was essentially created to fulfill obligations to the record label, with Lydon speedily snarking, "We only wanted to finish the album with the minimum amount of effort, which we are now doing very successfully." The rest of the time Lydon grunts, belches, manically talks to himself, and repetitively and hysterically wails: "We only wanted to be loved," in high contrast to the relatively laidback bassline and snare backbeat. Reynolds quotes Jah Wobble as saying that "Fodderstompf" has "got quite a sense of anarchy. In its own way, it's as mental as Funkadelic. And it had the perfect funk bassline."[57] In its lyrical and musical juxtapositions, "Fodderstompf" ironizes itself while poking fun at the record industry and cult of celebrity.

Simon Reynolds also reports that "[a]round this time Lydon started telling the press that the only contemporary music he really cared for was disco, a striking rhetorical move given the fact that the standard punk stance was that disco sucked. PiL, he stressed, were a *dance* band. Disco was functional, useful music."[58] These comments can be seen as yet another punk move in their contrariness, but as Lydon proved in an appearance on Capital Radio in 1977, where he demonstrated knowledge of dub in selecting records from his own collection, he was also genuinely a fan of music beyond what was expected of a punk artist.

Following the release of *Public Image*, PiL put out "Death Disco" on a twelve-inch that included two extended disco-mix versions, the "1/2 Mix" and the "Megga Mix," the title of the song explicitly pointing to their nihilistic take on dance music. Lydon howls and yelps his way through lyrics about the recent death of his mother as Wobble's bass pumps syncopation under a strained, ropey guitar version of the melody from Tchaikovsky's "Swan Theme." ("Death Disco" would reappear on *Metal Box* as "Swan Lake.") Lydon's scabrous vocals work in tandem with Levene's wall of metallic guitar textures to rasp against the funkiness of the underlying rhythm, generating a dance of high tension and paranoia. Their sound is the equivalent of chewing tin foil, rather than taking Quaaludes, on the discotheque floor.

Gang of Four

The other, more accessibly funky, major British dance-punk band of the first wave is Gang of Four, who, on top of being more accessible, were one of the most noticeable influences on later dance-punk, and punk and rock at large. Vocalist Jon King, guitarist Andy Gill, drummer Hugo Burnham, and bassist Dave Allen became a band while they were all living in Leeds. The former three were students at Leeds University, whose art department included members of the conceptual art group Arts & Language, which started in 1967 and was originally based around the journal *Art-Language*.

The Arts & Language group largely critiqued modernism and minimalism, promoting text-based art over painting and sculpture. This artistic criticism reinforced some of the band members' earlier interactions with art, including King's teenage exposure to Alfred Willener's *The Action-Image of Society: On Cultural Politicization*, which included examples of the Situationist International concept of *detournement*, a method that modifies existing texts in order to critique them alongside larger socioeconomic and sociopolitical issues.[59] This academic context provided Gang of Four with a way to interrogate and *detourne* both rock and dance music by combining them along with lyrical commentary on the contradictions of life under late capitalism.

According to Jim Dooley's history of Gang of Four, *Red Set*, the band's early musical interests ranged across record labels like Motown, Trojan, and Island, and artists such as Hawkwind, The Who, the Band, Bob Dylan, David Bowie, and the Velvet Underground and Nico. However, once punk began making headway in the UK, the original three members, King, Gill, and Burnham, posted a "bass player wanted" sign in the Leeds University Union Building that used the punk-influenced code "fast rivvum and blues band."[60] Allen, whose bass playing was inspired by jazz, funk, and reggae artists like Jaco Pastorius, Bootsy Collins, and Aston "Family Man" Barrett, answered the call. Allen ended up being the perfect, and necessary, fit because he could move beyond the limited rhythmic structures of punk, allowing the group to incorporate the sounds of funk and dub in what Jon King saw as "an attempt to end … the 'musical apartheid' of the mid-1970s—the sense that there were clear divisions between 'black music' and 'white music.'"[61]

In fact, King, who with the other members of the group frequented the reggae clubs in the Leeds suburb of Chapeltown, delighted in violating this line between race and gender as a dancing white man. He told Jim Dooley,

> It was quite good; all the best-looking girls liked us because we just loved dancing … That was the reason we liked reggae music, that and funk; it was dancing … So we'd get up there and all these boring students would sort of leave the floor when, you know, "Sex Machine" and "Double Barrel" and "Skinhead Moonstomp" would come on.[62]

The band's love of dancing would also see them listening to Chic, Funkadelic, and Michael Jackson's *Off the Wall*.

In their attempt to fuse punk with funk and dub while keeping to a socialist-inspired equity, Gang of Four did not have a conventional rhythm guitarist setup. Instead, Gill "would play in a style that was part rhythm, part lead, and part silence."[63]

The egalitarian sharing of space between all instruments ensured that "the vocals and music would interlock in a grid-like manner,"[64] or as Gill would later tell Dooley, a "Swiss watch of a rhythm."[65] Because of this non-aleatory, systematically planned approach (songs were mapped out on paper beforehand), Gang of Four's process was unlike PiL's sense of chaotic experimentalism.

One can hear this deliberate precision throughout Gang of Four's 1979 debut *Entertainment!*, which came out on EMI after the band had released their *Damaged Goods EP* on the independent Fast Records. In his review of the album, Jon Savage writes: "Spare and stark: over a dynamic, fluid, occasionally disco-inflected rhythm section, Gill's guitar is everywhere—driving the beat, chorded, or slashing in discordant shards, breaking the beat up without bringing everything to a grinding halt."[66]

He also comments on the lyrics of songs like "Not Great Men," "At Home He's a Tourist," "Glass," and "Natural's Not In It," emphasizing the intelligence at work in critiquing the complicity of people in the alienating, profit-driven capitalist system, perpetual consumers who cannot escape its logic even within intimate relationships and leisure time. The sense of estrangement in the lyrics is compounded by other alienating effects such as the competing and sometimes overlapping vocal lines of King and Gill, the strongest example being "Anthrax," in which Gill recites an analysis of the use of love in popular music at the same time as King sings about love making him feel like a beetle on its back, infected with anthrax.

In their first *New Musical Express* feature in 1978, the members of the band stress "how they want their followers to simultaneously think and dance."[67] It is this double-pronged intent that had several critics at the time wondering whether the "thinking" part of the equation did not always hit its mark because of the complexity of the lyrics, which were often based in academic theory and not readily apparent to working-class audiences.[68] Others, such as Mary Harron and Greil Marcus, were more open and celebratory of Gang of Four's forays into intellectual content. Harron makes a comparison to punk, which by this time had become an artistic cul-de-sac:

> Two years ago, when punk was still a living force, passion and disruption and self-expression were the values of the day. And because punk was, quite genuinely, an attack on privilege, it rejected the avant-garde as elitist, and disco as a symbol of record-company power.
>
> Well, the river moves on. Today punk is dead, the avant-garde has emerged as a powerful force and disco is considered to be the music of the people. Socialism has replaced anarchy, and theory is no longer despised: "structure" and "ideology" have replaced "frustration" and "energy" as the most over-used words in the rock press.[69]

In this excerpt, Harron is also referring to a shift in the discourse of British music journalism at the end of the 1970s, in which writers like Paul Morley and Ian Penman began to embrace critical theory and apply it to the popular music of the day. Marcus, who compared Gang of Four's relatively chaotic live performances with their recordings, writes, "The songs are gnomic, situational renderings of the paradoxes of leisure as oppression, identity as product, sex as politics; the theme here is not Armageddon (as, with the same material, it seemed to be onstage), but false consciousness within consumer culture."[70]

The false consciousness Marcus observes is also part of the strategy in using danceable music to convey dense political and socioeconomic ideas. Ultimately, the split in the reception to Gang of Four implies a class divide, though even academics queried the band's "limits of cultural critique," especially in the contradictions inherent to assuming a neo-Marxist stance while being on a major record label.[71]

Delta 5

Emerging from the same Leeds University art scene, Delta 5 is often seen as a sister band to Gang of Four with a similar dance-punk sound—or as rock critic Fred Mills illustrated it in 2006, "coruscating guitar, revolving bass line, Chic-styled beat and tribal-chant vocals as irresistible as early Go4."[72] Once described as "Rough Trade artsy-feminist Leedsites,"[73] Delta 5 featured Julz Sale on vocals and guitar, Allan Riggs on guitar, Kelvin Knight on drums, and notably, two bass players, Ros Allen and Bethan Peters.

Echoing Gang of Four's modus operandi, Riggs explained Delta 5's approach: "There had to be a groove and the lyrics had to mean something."[74] Thus, like Gang of Four, their lyrics have a critical depth, but with a focus on feminism. As Reynolds observes, "The women in Delta 5 … often wrote from a standpoint of defiance, aloofness, self-assertiveness, and unapproachable autonomy."[75] "Mind Your Own Business," Delta 5's most famous song and an exemplar of the cold, yet funny, indifference of the band, has a memorable bassline that bears a resemblance to The Slits' cover of "I Heard It through the Grapevine," flipping the paranoia and clinging sentiment into a song about refusal to engage in such rumor mongering. Speaking in 1980, Julz Sale explains the lyrics of another of their singles, "Alone," which, like "Mind Your Own Business," pushes the assumed partner or potential lover away, accelerating as it goes from a sullen, slow declaration to a fever-pitched shout and then back down again: "Sometimes you do want to go to bed alone without any explanations like 'I'm having my period' or 'I want to wash my hair.' Personal space and all that shit."[76]

As much as this prickly indifference defines the lyrical matter of Delta 5, the music itself, with its doubled guitars and basses, generates a sense of rhythmic dialogue. Riggs was drawn to the band because of the "potential scope for the guitar" saying at the time, "It can be conversational. It's nothing to do with playing chords all the way through like punk is. That's pretty boring."[77]

Reviewing a Delta 5 gig at the London Rock Garden in 1980, Phil Sutcliffe emphasized the danceability of their sound in contrast to punk. He observed that "the crowd pogo'd. Not that it was any throwback to punk. It's just the only thing you can do if you're in a confined space like that and the music insists on you dancing."[78] He goes on to note that despite certain features (dryness, sparsity, flat vocals), Delta 5 is still playing a form of disco that stands apart from other post-punk of the period: "Listen and what you hear is disco. A post-neutron-bomb mutation I dare say, but it's there in those two basses and Kelv's drums. With all their modern English aridity of stark arrangements, sparse crashing guitar and generally deadpan vocals, Delta 5 are musically more closely related to say Jermaine Jackson's 'Let's Get Serious' than the Fall's latest."[79]

After releasing several singles through Rough Trade, Delta 5 put out their one and only album, *See the Whirl*, in 1981. Unfortunately, it was deemed to be plagued by overproduction and brought their career to an early end. In comments made to Fred Mills, it seems the band realized that the minimalism of their sound was compromised with

Alan Riggs saying, "There is a bit of a 'kitchen sink' quality to the LP—sometimes experiments throw up good results, sometimes they don't."[80]

Au Pairs

Though based in Birmingham, England, Au Pairs is often included in the Gang of Four-Delta 5 milieu due to their similar sound and sense of politics, although they "were less intellectual Marxist, more instinctive female agitators."[81] Greil Marcus wrote about the similarities between the three bands:

> All of these bands derive some of their energy from an opposition to the attempt of a right-wing government to reorganize their society, and some from a commitment to dance music. All work from a fundamentally Jamaican aesthetic, in which musical (and, in a band that includes both women and men, sexual) hierarchy is bypassed … All are attuned to dub, the reggae form in which instruments and voices continually drop out of a song and then reappear in slightly different shape. The message conveyed is that of a sense of possibility and contingency opposed to—sometimes fighting off—a sense of fatalism.[82]

Including both Lesley Woods and Paul Foad on vocals and guitar, Jane Munro on bass, and Pete Hammond on drums, the Au Pairs' even gender split paralleled the title of their debut 1981 album, *Playing with a Different Sex*. Of course, the title also signals a potential fluidity and flux in both identity and relationships, some violent, some absurd, some knowing, which are explored across songs like "It's Obvious," "Repetition," and "We're So Cool." Characterizing the bitterness heard in

Lesley Woods's voice, Greil Marcus observes that the "male and female characters she sings through or about may be victims, but the distance her words and the Au Pairs' music establish between Woods and her characters, and that acrid tone, make it clear that people are perfectly capable of exchanging will and thought for life as a social fact."[83]

A Certain Ratio

As these British dance-punk bands gained popularity, they began touring the United States, including playing New York venues like Hurrah, Danceteria, the Mudd Club, The Ritz, and AM/PM. In his *Village Voice* article, "England's New Slant on Soul," Vince Aletti wrote, "instead of coming from Eurodisco strongholds in Germany, Italy, or France, the best imports right now are from England, where a peculiar confluence of styles— rap; reggae; power pop; fusion jazz; a cool, raceless R&B; plus a subversive touch here and there of new wave anarchy and irony—has produced an especially vivid and appealing brand of post-disco dance music."[84] The admiration was mutual as British music magazines sent their writers to New York to document the emergence of a parallel dance-punk scene. In some cases, British bands ended up recording there. One such band that stayed in New York to make their debut album was A Certain Ratio.

Formed around Peter Terrell on guitar and electronics and Simon Topping on vocals and trumpet, but quickly joined by bass guitarist/vocalist Jez Kerr and guitarist/trumpeter Martin Moscrop, A Certain Ratio was part of the stable of artists at Manchester's Factory Records that also included Joy Division. Along with other post-punk bands playing Factory club nights,

A Certain Ratio could be viewed as "both 'intellectual' and 'danceable,'"[85] though they initially retained darker, more difficult tones when compared with other dance-punk bands like New York's Liquid Liquid (more on them later). In his 1981 review of a Liquid Liquid show for *The Boston Globe*, Jim Sullivan observes how the Brits on the bill had a decidedly more serious approach than their Yankee counterparts: "A Certain Ratio approaches music as an almost arduous task. They're a funk band in a sense, but their execution and sound is [*sic*] determinedly grim—no joy in the industrial world. That may be an important message, but the music wears the listener down."[86]

This ambivalent, monochrome grimness or "funk noir,"[87] which was a staple of the Factory sound (see bands like Section 25 and Crispy Ambulance), was apparent on A Certain Ratio's 1980 compilation *The Graveyard and The Ballroom*. But the Mancunian group began shifting their groove while living in Tribeca to record their studio debut *To Each*. Glimpses of this more danceable sound could also be found on the persistent groove on the single "Do the Du (Casse)," which was paired with their cover of Banbarra's "Shack Up" from 1975. The latter featured a slightly less gloomy vocal from Topping, bolstered by jittery guitars and drunken brass.

Despite their name, A Certain Ratio often produced a less certain equation in practice. According to Martin Moscrop, their sound came from failing to imitate the electronic and funk music they were interested in at the time: "We were listening to so many different styles of music and searching for so many new things that, whatever we were listening to, we'd try and play—and it would come out the other end not sounding the same as the music we were trying to play, because we weren't proficient American musicians, we were ex-punks."[88]

Over the course of making *To Each*, the band added American vocalist Martha "Tili" Tilson. As Simon Reynolds explains, Tilson "gradually eclipsed" Topping, singing most tracks on 1982's *Sextet*. According to Reynolds, Topping had "lost confidence in his vocals and instead took lessons in hand percussion, an obsession ACR developed from watching Puerto Ricans playing congas in Central Park."[89] This lineup only recorded one more album, *I'd Like To See You Again*, before founding members Topping and Terrell left the band.

In *Rip It Up*, Simon Reynolds posits that the post-punk vanguard, which includes the dance-punk of PiL, Gang of Four, Delta 5, Au Pairs, and A Certain Ratio did not particularly succeed with dance music audiences. He argues that "for all their experiments with funk," these bands "really made music for 'heads' at home, not bodies on the floor."[90]

Reminiscent of Jim Sullivan's assessment of A Certain Ratio versus Liquid Liquid, Reynolds contends that what came to be called "mutant disco," a label attached to American bands like the B-52's, ESG, and Liquid Liquid, managed a more playful and danceable feel. However, the kitsch-obsessed B-52's, who would eventually fall under the new wave genre, did not initially succeed due to their dance-punk leanings: "One reason they didn't make it straightaway [*sic*] was that underneath the campy surface the B-52's' sound was stark and spiky, a tough dance groove midway between James Brown's minimal Afro-funk and the Leeds agit-funk of Gang of Four and Delta 5."[91]

Cross-Atlantic Cross-Pollination

Just as post-punk encompassed dance-punk artists under its umbrella, the mutant disco genre out of the New York music scene also involved several bands that could be classified as dance-punk. This "mongrel" scene, documented in Tim Lawrence's *Life and Death on the New York Dance*

Floor, flourished in parallel with the British dance-punk movement. And in a similar way to punk before it, dance-punk sounds cross-pollinated between the Big Apple and the UK. Furthermore, the 1978–84 New York scene produced its own "crosstown traffic"[92] between various writers, dancers, visual artists, filmmakers, and musicians, chipping away at the genre balkanization that had become the norm. Just as disco continued to peak underground at the Paradise Garage and the Saint into the early 1980s,[93] venues like the Mudd Club, the Roxy, and the Funhouse "encouraged musical conversations between uptown black and Latino kids and downtown white kids."[94]

This animated exchange leads Tim Lawrence to call the early 1980s "one of the most creatively vibrant and socially dynamic periods in the history of New York."[95] Lawrence's core arguments regarding the period assert that New York experienced a profound cultural renaissance made possible by the deindustrialization of the city and a community-driven party culture.[96] Over this time dance-punk found its spaces in the Mudd Club, Club 57, Danceteria, the Paradise Garage, and Funhouse, and found its networks through two independent record labels, ZE and 99.

These clubs all had different atmospheres—the Mudd Club as a Tribeca "disco for punks" modeled on Mère Vipère in Chicago;[97] Club 57 as a "groovy" East Village venue that had a more mid-century, B-movie, kitsch sensibility;[98] Danceteria as a multi-leveled midtown spot with simultaneous film screenings, live gigs, and dance floors; the Paradise Garage as a heaving, sweaty cavern of transcendent dance presided over by legendary DJ Larry Levan; and Funhouse as a Latino, freestyle dance zone, which was famously documented in New Order's music video for "Confusion."

Though there were still perceived divisions in some of these spaces—the Mudd Club as primarily a white art-punk space, the Paradise Garage as a Black gay club—the music being showcased often crossed genres and color lines. For example, at Danceteria DJs Sean Cassette and Mark Kamins played twelve-hour sets that allowed them "to explore contrasts and correspondences as they juxtaposed Public Image Ltd (PiL) and Bohannon, Killing Joke, and Donna Summer, while the fresh wave of recordings that started to layer punk sounds on top of a disco beat provided them with common ground."[99]

As Mark Kamins tells Tim Lawrence, "We could change the tempo but the vibe—the heart—would stay the same. The people that liked punk got into Bohannon and the people that were into my underground black music got into English punk and new wave because the vibe was the same."[100] And at the Mudd Club you could even find David Byrne of Talking Heads dancing to James Brown's "Hot Pants."[101]

From Avenue A to ZE: Dance-Punk Stateside

Talking Heads first emerged in the mid-1970s punk heyday of CBGB as a trio of former students from Rhode Island School of Design: David Byrne on vocals and guitar, Chris Frantz on drums, and Tina Weymouth on bass. A couple of years in, they added erstwhile Modern Lover, Jerry Harrison, on keyboards, guitar, and backing vocals.

Simon Reynolds distinguishes Talking Heads from the rest of the CBGB scene by asserting that they "always had a subtle funk pulse" and clarifying that this funk was "[n]ot in the 'passing for black' sense of, say, Scottish funkateers the Average White Band, but a more 'authentic' middle-class Caucasian take. You could hear the urge to get down, but checked and frustrated by an uptight WASPishness—a square and stilted quality Byrne physically embodied onstage with what Barney Hoskyns called his 'everything-is-so-normal-it's-crazy!' persona."[102]

This kind of nervy pulse can be found in early songs like "Psycho Killer" and "New Feeling," the latter borrowing the riff from the Marketts' "Out of Limits" but adding a layer of choppy vocals that evoke an existential pressure. Over the course of several more albums produced by Brian Eno, the funk influence became more pronounced (e.g., "Found a Job," "I Zimbra," "Life During Wartime," a cover of Al Green's "Take Me to the River"), culminating in the dance-punk sound of *Remain in Light* in 1980. In later interviews Byrne recounted how the band had been going to discos since their student days in Rhode Island and that their record collections mirrored their wider interests across genres, revealing that they listened to the Velvet Underground and Roxy Music alongside the soul and funk of Barry White, Parliament-Funkadelic, and The O'Jays and remarking, "We always thought there was really cool stuff going on in the discos."[103]

Simon Reynolds and Theo Cateforis explain the shift that brought Talking Heads to *Remain in Light* as a growing interest in Black music production techniques ("disco's extended remixes, the sumptuous layering, and thick textures of everyone from the Jacksons to Parliament-Funkadelic"[104]) and an equally increasing boredom with the fact that "every song revolved around a repetitious one- or two-chord groove."[105] Therefore, like other dance-punk bands, Talking Heads looked to Black music for a revolution in style that they didn't see in white styles like punk. It has also been said that Byrne was taking notes in the audience at early Gang of Four shows and that he keenly observed A Certain Ratio every night while on tour with them in the UK, demonstrating the expansion of the dance-punk sensibility.

In Cateforis's analysis of *Remain in Light*, he sees the influence of West African popular music but also an assimilation that was taken by critics at the time to be more authentic than it actually was. Cateforis maintains that even though the record had commonalities with West African pop, much of it was still indebted to Western rock music, including the use of backbeat and a constant duple framework along with a lack of true layered polyrhythms.[106]

Nonetheless, *Remain in Light* became their most successful record up to that time and foreshadowed their truly commercial hit album *Speaking in Tongues* (1983). To tour *Remain in Light*, Talking Heads expanded "to include a number of African American musicians (notably Bernie Worrell of Parliament/Funkadelic),"[107] but some contemporaries picked up on the issues that Cateforis outlines. Comparing *Remain in Light* to the Detroit band Was (Not Was) in 1981, ZE Records founder Michael Zilkha said that the former "doesn't ring true."[108]

James White and the Blacks

Michael Zilkha came from England to New York City in 1975, where he began frequenting the eclectic music scene. Though he wanted to review music for *The Village Voice*, he ended up writing theater reviews because of his inability to impress renowned music critic Robert Christgau. After a failed attempt to develop a record label with former Velvet Underground member John Cale, Zilkha founded ZE

Records with French producer Michel Esteban, who had made his fortune in selling clothing.

Zilkha himself came from a privileged background: his father founded the Mothercare chain in Britain and his stepfather was Labour Party politician and millionaire Harold Lever. Therefore, he had a trust fund to invest in the venture. Though Zilkha had a self-professed "white hippy sensibility," his label became known for "cool, sharp, weird, intelligent and funky" aesthetics that made it "so hip it hurts."[109] In July 1981, music journalist Peter Silverton compared Zilkha to his record label, describing them both as "small, intelligent, neurotic and well-dressed."[110]

Zilkha's vision for the label was grounded in a disco-punk fusion. In 2009, ZE producer and leader of Kid Creole and the Coconuts, August Darnell, reflected on the hybridity of ZE: "It was where Studio 54 met the Mudd Club. It should never have happened, but it did—the disco people usually looked down on the punks, but because of my obsession with eclecticism and Michael Zilkha's vision, those two worlds could co-exist."[111] Simon Reynolds quotes Luc Sante, a member of the downtown New York scene in the late 1970s and early 1980s, in describing ZE's "'potent formula' as 'anything at all + disco bottom.'"[112] It was particularly after seeing the no wave band James Chance and the Contortions perform that Zilkha was inspired, telling Paul Rambali in 1981, "It was right after Saturday Night Fever and I knew there had to be some sort of equivalent of dance music, and here it was!"[113]

James Chance (born James Siegfried) moved from his home city of Milwaukee to New York City to join the loft jazz scene—which "saw free jazz musicians gather in disused loft spaces like Studio We, Studio Rivbea and Ali's Alley that were owned by the musicians themselves in order to hone a seemingly structureless, searching sound that was dubbed 'ecstatic'"[114]—although, various factors curtailed his involvement, including the fact that "its white hipster and hippie contingents annoyed him too much"[115] and that "[h]is punk attitude chafed against the late-sixties mind-set of the predominantly black jazz milieu."[116] He played sax for a short time in Teenage Jesus and the Jerks, another no wave band led by Lydia Lunch, before eventually forming the Contortions, "a James Brown-inspired outfit with added atonality and sax solos,"[117] which "fused three great American musical extremists—Iggy Pop, James Brown, and Albert Ayler."[118]

The Contortions were one of four bands on Brian Eno's 1978 *No New York* compilation that ostensibly showcased "no wave," a genre that took punk to its nihilistic extreme and dispensed with conventional rhythms, structures, and tones. Chance has said, "I never felt like I was part of any real movement with those other bands, because my music was always much more danceable and not as arty."[119]

Zilkha proposed that Chance combine punk and disco, resulting in Chance's new band James White and the Blacks (originally and tellingly first proposed by Chance as James White and *His* Blacks). As Simon Reynolds recounts, "The sheer conceptual shock value of becoming a disco turncoat and fucking with everybody's heads grabbed Chance's imagination."[120] Chance and Anya Phillips, a fashion designer and cofounder of the Mudd Club who was Chance's partner and manager, both thrived on provocation in a similar vein as John Lydon; in a way, the punkest thing to do was to sell out and become punk's opposite.

Chance released his Contortions album, *Buy*, in the same year as *"Off White,"* his record with James White and the Blacks. Reynolds notes the difference between the two, with the former representing the "unsustainable intensity of the early scene, and the chic, sleek *Off White* pointed ahead toward 'mutant disco'" and "disco punk."[121] Tim Lawrence also hails *"Off White"* as the "arrival of a fresh punk-funk sound"[122] that featured a reworking of "Contort Yourself" from *Buy*.

August Darnell was responsible for the remix of "Contort Yourself," which sanded off some of the sharpest edges, brought in more space, and introduced a prominent melodic bassline. Speaking to Tim Lawrence, Zilkha remarked that "[a]lthough James White and the Blacks were meant to be a disco band, it wasn't until that remix that the vision was truly realized."[123] As the title of the record makes clear, as well as the tracks "Almost Black" and "Bleached Black," this music existed in ironic quotation marks and foregrounded a "failed" authenticity in incorporating elements of Black music into Chance's blasé whiteness. This inauthenticity was highlighted with the record launch party hosted by ZE, featuring Chance and his band lip-synching and dressed in 1960s soul singer attire, backed by two teenage dancers called the "Disco Lolitas."

Bush Tetras

The other notable record label producing dance-punk in this period was 99 (pronounced "nine-nine"), which emerged from 99 Records, a store on MacDougal Street in Greenwich Village. The shop was originally opened in 1978 by Gina Franklyn, a British clothing designer who sold punk clothing and accessories. When Brooklynite DJ and soundman Ed Bahlman became Franklyn's boyfriend, he began working at the store and started selling punk and no wave records and British imports. Customers included Thurston Moore, Rick Rubin, and Vivien Goldman, who recalls that the "store used to function a bit like the old Rough Trade shop, where it was very much also a milieu or salon where people would hang out and you'd have an exchange of ideas."[124] Similarly, Mike Rubin describes 99 as a cross "between an American answer to the British label Rough Trade and a punky precursor to DFA."[125]

Because of Franklyn's connection to England, there was an "Anglophile slant"[126] to 99 Records as a store and a label. For example, Bahlman, who produced many of the records 99 released, formed a reciprocal release agreement with British-based Y Records and collaborated with Adrian Sherwood's On-U Sound Records.[127] And one of his early releases by Bush Tetras shared a strong affinity with female-fronted dance-punk from the UK.

Bush Tetras, the band formed by guitarist Pat Place after quitting the Contortions, also included Cynthia Sley and Laura Kennedy, who dropped out of art school in Cleveland to move to New York. Place herself had come to New York from Chicago in 1975 to pursue performance and conceptual art, placing Bush Tetras' background in an analogous vein to bands like Gang of Four and Delta 5. Completing the lineup on drums was ex-*Creem* writer Dee Pop, who once interviewed Sex Pistols and The Clash.

At the time, critic Richard Grabel described their sound by writing, "The beat has echoes of the speedy, cracked funk of Gang of Four or PiL, while the songs range from menace to exaltation, bitter sarcasm to evocative love-shouts."[128] Their seven-inch EP *Too Many Creeps* became the third release on 99 in 1980 and received "significant airplay on WNEW-FM and in New York dance clubs," going on to sell nearly 30,000 copies.[129] With its nearly monotone bassline matching the dead flatness in Sley's vocals, "Too Many Creeps" declares the lack of safety, connection, and value of the public sphere of the streets: "I just don't wanna go/Out in the streets no more/ Because these people they give me/They give me the creeps." According to Vivien Goldman, "The first verse ... was written by Place in the ticket booth at the Bleecker Street Theatre, where she and Kennedy worked."[130]

Place tells Goldman, "We were freaks, and we would get hassled if we left the East Village—and even there."[131] Sley attributes this hassle to the fact that the band threatened and destabilized people's assumptions about gender: "We were pretty sassy and people were scared of us. We were attacked and had a hard time. With our short haircuts, people could not figure out if we were boys or girls."[132] "Too Many Creeps" would be their one and only release on 99 with the band moving to British label Fetish for subsequent singles and another EP, but Bahlman still had other dance-punk pioneers on his roster, namely, Liquid Liquid and ESG.

Liquid Liquid

Liquid Liquid developed out of the "primitive punk band" Liquid Idiot, which played venues such as CBGB. Comprised of Sal Principato (vocals/percussion), Richard McGuire (bass), Scott Hartley (drums), and Dennis Young (marimba), Liquid Liquid was named as such because it "suggested a slippery grooviness."[133] Their self-titled debut EP "combined the Bo Diddley beat, the rototoms in Curtis Mayfield's 'Super Fly,' the percussive crescendos of Fela Kuti, the subtractive spatial dimension of dub reggae, and the deconstructive rock of DNA."[134]

Speaking to *Clash Magazine* in 2010, Principato says, "from our perspective we wanted to make groovy music, music to make you move, to make your body sing. But you know, dance music was disco then. And you know, I love disco, I spin disco all the time but we didn't want to be a disco act, we felt a million miles away from that."[135] At the same time, Principato sees Liquid Liquid's material as being more aptly described as "deconstructed rock" than post-punk, or "[r]ock that wasn't expanding but breaking itself down, which led us to dub reggae, which led us to anything that was like skeletal, or stripped down but with more emotional content than actual bulk."[136]

In addition to the influence of dub, Liquid Liquid heavily relied on Latin percussion. Speaking to Simon Reynolds, Richard McGuire described the influence of their environment on their sound: "The Lower East Side of Manhattan was very Hispanic and you heard this Latin stuff all the time coming out of every bodega. All of our cowbell and conga sounds were coming from being exposed to that."[137] McGuire also saw the nascent hip-hop scene as an inspiration: "It wasn't till I heard Grandmaster Flash's 'Wheels of Steel' for the first time that I thought *that was the future.*"[138]

According to Principato, their composition process was organic, explaining, "If one instrument expressed itself confidently, then the rest of us would follow its lead—but generally we'd work a groove until something emerged. That said often drums and bass would be the anchor."[139] A unique feature among dance-punk at the time, Liquid Liquid did not often have discernible lyrics with Principato using his voice as another element of percussion or atmospheric texture. At a show in Boston in 1981, the vocalist explained their lyrical approach: "It's done for impact, the emotion behind it. They're not really that decipherable. It evokes the subconscious."[140]

Liquid Liquid went on to release two more EPs on 99, *Successive Reflexes* (1981) and *Optimo* (1983), with Ed Bahlman regularly giving the acetates of Liquid Liquid's music to his brother Bill, who was a DJ in the West Village, to test them out on audiences.[141] Like their labelmates ESG, Liquid Liquid was one of the few dance-punk acts to be truly embraced by the gay Black and Latino scene at clubs like Paradise Garage, as well as the more heterosexual Latino scene at Funhouse.

Simon Reynolds relates how McGuire would often hand-deliver Liquid Liquid EPs to "resident DJ god, Larry Levan" at Paradise Garage.[142] McGuire tells Reynolds, "The Garage was an insane place. It really was a big parking garage that was turned into a disco. When we played, they had us do three songs, then get offstage. This was typical for all these big dance places we played, like the Funhouse, or the Roxy. It was so much more about the DJ."[143] The crossing of color lines in Liquid Liquid's oeuvre eventually translated into a defining moment for the band and their record label.

Their last EP for 99 contained "Cavern," arguably Liquid Liquid's most famous song with its memorable two-note bassline and Principato's repeated chant of "Slip in and out of phenomenon." Its underground popularity caught the attention of artists at the hip-hop label Sugar Hill, and shortly after, Grandmaster Flash and Melle Mel released "White Lines (Don't Do It)," an anti-cocaine track that changed Principato's "slip in and out of phenomenon" to "something like a phenomenon" and replicated McGuire's bassline by using bassist Doug Wimbish of the Sugar Hill house band to play it. Technically not a sample, but also undeniably a copy, "White Lines (Don't Do It)" became the unprecedented legal gray area to end two independent record labels, an event that would also come to negatively affect Liquid Liquid's labelmates ESG.

ESG

ESG, which stands for Emerald, Sapphire, and Gold, consisted of the four Scroggins sisters from the Bronx—Valerie on drums, Deborah on bass, Renée on vocals, and Marie on congas—in addition to their friend Tito Libran also on congas. As Vivien Goldman observes, ESG emerged from a New York neighborhood portrayed as dangerous and tumultuous in the public eye: "The Scroggins family was caught up in the regular infernos captured in the 1972 BBC documentary *The Bronx is Burning* … Often set for insurance, uptown's wanton arson and carnage occurred amid manipulated violence from gangs and drugs—coke, crack, angel dust."[144] Famously, the Scroggins' mother encouraged her daughters to take up music as a way to keep them safe from the risks endemic in their community.

Ed Bahlman discovered ESG when they lost a talent search sponsored by CBS Records, for which he was a judge. Simon Reynolds describes ESG as a "cross between Public Image and Tamla Motown" and argues that their "odd mixture of emaciated minimalism and raw soul, their hard-funk basslines and chittering percussion, totally fit postpunk notions of what dance music should be."[145] Tim Lawrence compares ESG to James Brown and his band in terms of their slow builds: "Developing instrumental parts that emulated and extended the funk jams demanded by Brown after he took the J.B.'s to the bridge, with lyrics introduced only after the track's dynamics were in place, ESG's players came to think of themselves as a dance band."[146] This process of extension also related significantly to the way the new hip-hop scene in ESG's borough was manipulating turntables to lengthen the rhythm breakdown sections of funk and R&B songs.[147]

In an article from the *New Musical Express* in 1981, Richard Grabel writes, "ESG don't play fake anything. ESG play real funk, transformed their own way into something direct, unfussy, irresistible. They make original rhythms, stripped down to the bare bones."[148] When Grabel mentions that some have called ESG "minimalist salsa" (an adjective that likely came from the assumption that ESG were Puerto Rican though they had a multi-racial background of African American, Cherokee, Irish, and Italian), Renée responds, "Salsa is more hot." Grabel suggests, "Your music is more cool," and Renée confirms while giggling, "We like to think of it that way. Cool." The implication of being cool rather than hot relates to a sense of self-mastery, emotional control, and economy, as well as a source of underground cultural capital, which ESG continues to be among musicians, DJs, and music fans.

Because of the extended, but sparse, rhythms, their songs "Moody" and "UFO" became some of the most sampled tracks in house and hip-hop. Sharing an appeal to non-white audiences with Liquid Liquid, ESG were invited to play at Paradise Garage on New Year's Eve 1981 and alongside the Peech Boys for Larry Levan's birthday in 1982. David DePino, another DJ who worked at Paradise Garage, spoke of Levan's admiration for ESG: "It sounded like a garage band. It sounded raw. ESG were obscure and Larry loved obscure."[149]

ESG also became a staple of the scene that embraced British dance-punk. After opening for A Certain Ratio at Hurrah, Factory Records offered them an opportunity to record a seven-inch single (including "You're No Good," "UFO," and "Moody") with their in-house producer Martin Hannett, renowned for developing the Factory post-punk sound, especially with Joy Division. 99 subsequently released their own EP of the same three tracks with three additional live cuts. Eventually, ESG would play the opening night of the Haçienda, the Manchester club opened by Factory in 1982. The Haçienda, inspired by the early 1980s clubs in New York as experienced by co-owners New Order, would come to stage a different wave of indie rock and dance hybrids in the latter half of the decade. With ESG's connections to Factory and the British dance-punk scene, the eclectic new genre had come full circle.

In the early 1980s, as the CBGB punk scene was running out of energy, the post-punk dance scene that followed also began to wane. Tim Lawrence pinpoints the decline of the dance-punk scene as beginning in 1982, when "a number of the no wave and punk-funk lineups that had charged the city's live music scene with angular and groove-oriented possibilities struggled to match the searing impact of their breakthrough efforts,"[150] with less critical fervor for *Sax Maniac* by James White and the Blacks and ESG's EP *ESG Says Dance to the Beat of Moody*.

The novelty of dance-punk had, in part, begun to wear off, and bands were disappearing either due to lack of interest or by becoming too successful for the underground scene, with Mudd Club owner Steve Mass using Gang of Four as an example of a band they could no longer afford to book.[151] Lawrence recounts that the summer of 1983 in New York

> turned out to be awkwardly quiet on the live band front, and although ESG livened up the autumn with their debut album, *Come Away with ESG*, which the *New York Times* reviewed as being "as rigorously minimal as anything in SoHo and as tough as anything uptown," the release didn't stop *Dance Music Report* from bemoaning the 'formularization' of dance-oriented rock.[152]

The same year would see Mudd Club and Club 57 close.

In 1984, ZE Records wound down while 99 Records and Liquid Liquid ceased altogether, the former having gone bankrupt from suing Sugar Hill over copyright infringement for "White Lines." Despite having won the lawsuit, 99 did not receive any of the $660,000 owed because Sugar Hill filed for bankruptcy protection and went defunct two years later. The members of Liquid Liquid would only begin earning royalties on their sampled material after Duran Duran covered "White Lines" in 1995,[153] and Ed Bahlman would retreat from the music scene for good, leaving artists like ESG without legal recourse or access to their master tapes.

Lawrence cites various changes in government policies as ultimately shutting down the New York scene that birthed dance-punk, including "reductions in government spending and welfare, the deregulation of the banking sector, tax cuts for the wealthy, and the introduction of additional tax breaks to stimulate corporate investment in the city."[154] Danceteria closed in 1986 and Paradise Garage one year later while New York club life became ground zero for the AIDS epidemic. In the UK, indie musical trends moved in a New Pop direction as MTV made former post-punk artists into global superstars and even dance-punk pioneers like Gang of Four took up drum machines and synths.

Simon Reynolds argues that this period also saw a shift in music journalism: "More than musical inspiration per se, what began to sink into a coma was the *discourse* around music."[155] In his view, music journalists of the first dance-punk period "played a big role in terms of championing certain bands or scenes, pushing particular directions for music, and making a set of values and a particular kind of language and way of thinking about music seem 'sexy.' ... Nowadays this oracular notion of the rock writer has faded away."[156] With new colorful magazines like *The Face* and *Smash Hits* gaining traction over the "inkies" like the *New Musical Express*, *Melody Maker*, and *Sounds*, journalism went from poststructuralist to postmodern, poking fun at its own superficiality.

When dance-punk reemerged, it would be in response to an accumulated history of dance and punk music, alongside a new genre called indie.

3   Life Makes Echoes: Dance-Punk Dubbed in the Post-Punk Revival

Between the mid-1980s and early 1990s, dance music spread and circulated from various underground spaces across the United States and Europe, fracturing into numerous genres and subgenres that, despite their differences, were also heirs to those 1970s harbingers of the future, "Trans-Europe Express" and "I Feel Love,"[1] which had previously influenced first-wave dance-punk. Dance-punk like ESG and Liquid Liquid had a large impact on these new dance music deviations, while other dance-punk such as Gang of Four made its mark on 1980s and 1990s American suburban punks like Minutemen and Fugazi.[2]

However, these influences had become separated: dance became increasingly insular and specific, while punk retreated into grooveless and ever speedier thrash in angry response to the Reagan culture wars[3] before moving into the mainstream through grunge. While the dance scenes grew more hedonistic with the wide use of drugs like ecstasy, factions of punk became more ascetic, culminating in the straightedge subculture.

An exception to this genre divergence briefly flourished in the late 1980s at Manchester's Haçienda, the same Factory Records and New Order-financed club that first hosted dance-punk acts in the early 1980s. Dubbed Madchester, bands like The Stone Roses, Happy Mondays, and the Charlatans began playing indie rock influenced by the growing UK acid house scene. DJ and producer Andrew Weatherall was a key part of this period with his remixes of Happy Mondays and New Order and his production of Primal Scream's transformation from indie pop to rave on *Screamadelica*. The Haçienda seemingly inspired what is termed the "indie disco" in the UK, a type of club night that increased in popularity through the 1990s and the 2000s at which danceable indie rock and pop are played. Chamber pop outfit The Divine Comedy famously celebrates such a night in the 2010 song "At the Indie Disco," while Kieron Gillen and Jamie McKenzie's second Phonogram comic book series, *The Singles Club*, documents the magic of an indie disco circa 2006.

During this period the term "indie" came to define not only an independent method of record production and distribution, which had become a less meaningful idea given the increasing partnerships between major and independent labels,[4] but a progressively more catchall term for a predominantly white rock music that somehow didn't fit into the mainstream; sometimes because it was too low-fidelity and shambolic, sometimes because it largely appealed to university students, sometimes because it featured "jangly" guitars.

The indie artists and labels of the 1980s largely had their roots in the American and British DIY punk and post-punk scenes. In the UK, these indie labels included Rough Trade, Stiff Records, Factory, Good Vibrations, 4AD, Mute, Cherry Red, Creation, Sarah Records, and Heavenly, which all specialized in different subgenres of indie music or specific geographical regions, often cultivating their own visual styles. For example, 4AD focused on the oneiric, gothy sound of artists like Cocteau Twins and Dead Can Dance, while Sarah Records was associated with the twee indie pop that seemed to take their template wholesale from indie heroes The Smiths'"Cemetry Gates."

One of the most prominent events in British indie music history was the eclectic *C86* compilation cassette produced by the *New Musical Express*, which featured bands such as Primal Scream, The Wedding Present, and McCarthy, and eventually became shorthand for all indie that prided itself on underachievement, low-fidelity sound, and lack of musical ability. This indie scene set a precedent for what would follow, namely a dominantly "white" sound with "quirky" and "clever" lyrics that did not draw upon dance music styles originated by non-white artists. The closest The Smiths got to a groove was "Barbarism Begins at Home."

Meanwhile, American indie labels like Sub Pop, SST Records, Matador, Touch and Go, and K Records shared a philosophy of purism and authenticity with British indie but tended to have noisier, more confrontational rosters (Big Black, Sonic Youth, Dinosaur Jr., Butthole Surfers). As much as this music inhabited a visceral physicality, and sometimes sensory overload, the lack of danceability remained the same, with indie artists ostensibly equating such a characteristic with their antithesis: commercial pop music. By the early 1990s, perhaps in response to the mainstreaming of grunge, American indie rock took a lo-fi turn with bands like Pavement, Guided by Voices, Neutral Milk Hotel, and Sebadoh, sometimes perceived as a "grungier" grunge for Generation X.

As punk broke into the mainstream via grunge in the United States, indie rock entered the mainstream in the UK. This "new" guitar-based music reacted to grunge—and the American dominance it represented—by looking to the 1960s British Invasion, and to some extent early 1970s British glam, for inspiration and added a dash of regional detail. The oft-cited origin of this music scene is the April 1993 issue of *Select Magazine*, which featured a cover with Brett Anderson, lead singer of Suede, posing over a Union Jack background and the headline "Yanks go home!" This "new" indie paralleled the rise of an equally suspect "new" Labour party and was dubbed Britpop.

For a few years London swung again, and Britannia was cool with bands like Suede, Blur, Oasis, Elastica, and Pulp leading the charge. However, just as the "third way" of New Labour quickly lost its buoyant appeal, Britpop hit a hard comedown, and the indie music that still existed became more esoteric in genres like post-rock, which had taken shoegaze to its logical extreme. Grunge, too, burned out *and* faded away with Kurt Cobain's suicide and the ensuing years of homogenous alternative rock. In the woozy hangover, manufactured teenage pop rushed in to fill the vacuum, becoming the last real cash cow for the severely consolidated music industry before the advent of the MP3 file, Napster, and the iPod.

"Well, How Did I Get Here?": The Early 2000s

To understand how dance-punk came back to life, it's important to understand what the world looked like in the early 2000s. At the turn of the millennium, an anti-climactic Y2K was followed by the terrorist attacks of September 11, kicking off the war on terror led by George W. Bush and Tony Blair that defined the first half of the decade. The time felt both bleak and nondescript, as demonstrated by David Wilkinson's description of the music world in 2001: "*NME*'s predictions for that year were a motley collection of stale post-Britpop bands, US nu-metal imports and the dying embers of 1990s dance."[5]

And indie music snobbery only grew as record collector nerds' one-upmanship could reach nuclear levels with increasing access to digitized back catalogs and crowdsourced music databases like *Discogs*.

The neoliberalism that had grown up through the 1980s and outlived the Cold War had become the only reality, rendering identity in the West both profoundly important from the perspective of a competitive subject and deeply fungible in the view of post-identity politics. For the neoliberal individual, it felt as though one desperately needed an identity to stand out in the ever globalizing, deindustrialized market. The strident politics of previous generations no longer applied in what many saw as a postfeminist, post-racial, postmodern world. The sense of lateness implied by "post" didn't really inspire ideas about the future; instead, it created an intense worry about catching up to the present and a desire to relinquish the possibility of originality.

The arrival of the Internet only exacerbated the feeling that too much history had already happened and this was as good as it was going to get, at least in the West. There were no more grand narratives to be written. Language, and thus reality, had been determined to be subjective, relative, and unstable. The ineffectual 1999 protests against the World Trade Organization and the 2003 protests against the Iraq War did little to quell political apathy and futility. This malaise also speaks to the growing privileged class of young people who saw their identity as increasingly mutable. How do you seek some form of authenticity and value when you know that authenticity is always compromised and value changes quickly?

By presumably leveling the playing field, liberal democracy, postmodernism, and the "democratizing" Internet had also flattened difference and the ability to form authentic subcultures or original art. Digital culture, which can be easily and exactly reproduced, made copying a way of life, further complicating ideas about authenticity. The question of what constituted original, new, or valuable art—previously debated in the 1960s and 1970s by groups like the Gang of Four-influencing Art & Language—was once again a major source of anxiety.

In response to such anxieties, people developed strategies to produce value and set themselves apart, including curating existing materials and experiences and turning consumer tastes into an entrepreneurial endeavor.

The Elevation of the Curator

Art critic David Balzer argues that during this period, the concept of a curator evolved from the role of a subservient and responsive "caretaker" to that of a respected connoisseur whose job it is "to make sense of things, to act as advocate for an ever more obtuse, factionalist art scene."[6] Balzer coined the term *curationism*, "a play on *creationism*, with its cultish fervour and its adherence to divine authorship and grand narratives," to define what he saw as "the acceleration of the curatorial impulse to become a dominant way of thinking and being."[7]

He pinpoints this shift to the mid-1990s and argues that we are now living in "the curationist moment," dominated by a reliance on credentialed experts to generate value, and therefore audiences and markets, through the reorganization of cultural texts.[8] In turn, Balzer suggests that these audiences and consumers are increasingly engaged in curating their own identities to make meaning and grant value to their lives.[9] He links this everyday curationism to an increase in unpaid or minimally paid affective labor, as well as volunteer work performed in the pursuit of one's own interests. Affective labor, sometimes used interchangeably with immaterial labor, became a dominant form of work after deindustrialization in the West, where people are no longer manufacturing products but supplying services that are meant to affect the emotions and feelings of those being served, trading in communication, information, and networks. This kind of labor, which can build and bolster one's own identity and cultural capital, can be seen in the MP3 blogs of the 2000s and the curated Spotify playlists of today. This constant need to curate stems from an anxiety to impose control, order, and value on an ever more saturated and trivial information economy.[10] If everything is important, ultimately nothing is. At the same time, being highly versed in intertextual references and trivia becomes currency in the knowledge economy of late capitalism.

The impulse to curate experiences appears in the music world in the form of album tours, on which older bands play their classic albums in full, often from start to finish. Another example is the phenomenon of "curated" festivals, such as Lollapalooza and All Tomorrow's Parties, through which musicians demonstrate their tastes by choosing the combination of bands in the lineup, often providing them an opportunity to highlight obscure acts and revive interest in older bands that sometimes even reunite for the festival. Balzer argues that "[t]hese phenomena can be inspiring as well as tedious; regardless, they are conspicuously, fundamentally anti-avant-garde. Their collective dictum might as well be 'Make it old.'"[11]

The Rise of the Hipster

One of Balzer's examples of curationism is Jim Jarmusch's 2013 film *Only Lovers Left Alive,* which stars Tom Hiddleston and Tilda Swinton as über-connoisseur vampires who speak not only to the elevation of the curationist but also the rise of the hipster. Metaphorical vampires, "real hipsters are *not* artists. They're curators and critics, re-mixers and designers, the copywriters and 'prosumers' who trail in the artists' wake. At best, it seems they're art students: aspiring cultural savants who collect the names and slogans of past avant-gardes to hoard or brandish conspicuously, like capital."[12]

The oft-maligned figure of the 2000s hipster became such a conspicuous element of global consumer culture that in 2009 literary journal *n+1* organized a panel discussion attempting to define it. It resulted in a publication called *What Was the Hipster?*, in which *n+1* editor Mark Greif gives three potential definitions: the "white hipster," that which belongs to "hipster culture," and "the hip consumer."[13]

Associated with *Vice* magazine, American Apparel, trucker hats, and The Strokes, the "white hipster" fetishizes lower-middle-class suburban and rural whiteness in a seemingly ironic act of rebellion.[14] Greif's second definition, that of "hipster culture," draws on the arrested development or prolonged youth of hipster adults. Linked to Wes Anderson films, early writing of Dave Eggers, and Belle and Sebastian, this culture thrives on artistic work that is simultaneously knowing and naïve, both adult-like and childish. Greif sees this version of hipsterism as using irony apolitically, not to critique society but to access and revel in the emotional past of their childhoods.[15] The third definition, the "hip consumer," embodies subcultural capital on steroids as the accessibility and speed of the online world makes it increasingly difficult to stay ahead of what's hip or cool.[16] In Greif's view, the hip consumer is primarily an aficionado rather than a producer, echoing David Balzer's description of the curator.

According to Greif, the hipster is often such a despised figure because, unlike other subculture members, he "aligns himself *both* with rebel subculture *and* with the dominant class, and opens up a poisonous conduit between the two."[17] Or as Jake Kinzey has said, "[h]ipsters are *the* most postmodern 'mainstream-subculture' to date and are perfectly integrated into postmodern late-capitalism."[18] Others have referred to hipster culture as a "post-subcultural" one.[19] Greif describes this situation as arising from "a thwarted tradition of youth subcultures," in which the underground and alternative has "been integrated, humiliated, and destroyed."[20]

In the face of such futile struggle, hipsters ascribe to what is termed "cultural omnivorousness." First used as a term by Richard Peterson in order to better understand changes in music audience segmentation in the 1990s, cultural omnivorousness refers to the way elite classes have shifted to less hierarchical tastes, embracing what is considered high and low culture simultaneously.[21] In the hipster context, the question "'What kind of music do you like?' has become a tedious, unanswerable question."[22] Balzer remarks, "We hope our identities are more complex than that, and indeed desire them to be."[23]

The cultural omnivore was alive and well at the turn of the millennium as journalist John Heilemann testifies in Lizzy Goodman's oral history of the early 2000s New York rock scene, *Meet Me in the Bathroom*:

> I like Guns N' Roses and I like Tribe Called Quest and I like the Cure and the Smiths. It used to always make me crazy that somehow if you said you like this, you couldn't like that.

> In the aughts, everything stopped being quite so Bloods
> and Crips, Jets and Sharks. You could like Nas and LCD
> Soundsystem and the Strokes and people wouldn't look
> at you funny. No one would think that somehow that was
> unduly promiscuous. It's mashup culture.[24]

On the one hand, this kind of perspective seems analogous
to the 1970s and 1980s modernist impulse to put disco, funk,
dub, and punk together as a way to imagine a borderless
future. However, another possible way to interpret this attitude
is that of a "quest for perpetual cool … sustained by endless
cultural imperialism."[25]

Hipsters are often described using the language of
colonization, especially as they form the largely white face of
gentrification across the world's largest cities, including the
mythologized crucible of two waves of dance-punk, New York
City. It is in this context that the second wave of dance-punk
surfaces. David Wilkinson identifies how the post-punk revival,
of which the dance-punk revival is a strong component, began
to emerge in the first years of the new millennium through
compilations, reissues, Simon Reynolds's *Rip It Up*, themed club
nights, and new bands with post-punk's old sound. However,
he notes that the "revival's frequently explicit pastiche was
somewhat at odds with post-punk's emphasis on innovation.
Very few bands, too, displayed an interest in the oppositional
politics that often animated the original wave of post-punk."[26]
Wilkinson's assessment of the apolitical, superficial bent of
these newer bands resonates with Reynolds's conclusions in *Rip
It Up*, in which he questions their seemingly empty militancy.
He hypothesizes that this dearth of explicit political verve is
"not so much futile as difficult to do convincingly, given that
the nineties sensibility of irony and disengagement has yet to
relinquish its grip on the culture."[27]

There's much to unpack here, but both Wilkinson and Reynolds appear to base their judgment of second-wave dance-punk on the assumption that the bands of the late 1970s and early 1980s were both politically reactionary and progressive in the modern sense. There is also a supposition that post-punk bands of the new millennium *should* create and behave in the same way that the earlier ones did and that popular music needs to be teleologically progressive, or keep moving forward in a linear, goal-oriented fashion, in order to matter. Though bands like Gang of Four raised sociopolitical issues like false consciousness under capitalism, they also acknowledged their own complicity and inability to overcome the system. They, and others like Liquid Liquid, had grown tired of the seriousness and limitations of punk, and so they decided to dance.

By the late 1990s, punk, as well as its offspring indie rock, had again been recognized as a dead end in the face of an even more solidified neoliberal order. Meanwhile, moral panics about rave culture had once again vilified dance music for its permissive, hedonistic attitude. And like disco before it, it would once again be assimilated in the shift that got cross-armed rock kids to move their bodies.

Dance to the Underground: Dance-Punk's Rebirth in Brooklyn

It is during the first decade of the twenty-first century that the names dance-punk and disco-punk become assigned retroactively to music that was once called avant-funk, punk-funk, new wave, mutant disco, or post-punk. In April 2003,

Muzik published an issue with the feature article "Disco Punk Explosion!"[28] and an accompanying free CD called *Dance to the Underground*.

The article included interviews with personalities and bands associated with the new disco-punk scene in New York, including James Murphy and Tim Goldsworthy (who were then producing under the name The DFA), Radio 4, Liars, Out Hud, The Rapture, and The Juan Maclean. It also profiled some UK-based bands (Big Two Hundred, Gramme, Zongamin) and liberally sprinkled insets about the history and roots of disco-punk, such as ESG, Liquid Liquid, Gang of Four, PiL, and Talking Heads, formalizing the discursive connections.

Centered this time in the borough of Brooklyn, this new dance-punk scene, akin to the milieu of their Manhattan-based predecessors, contained a spectrum of sounds that ranged from the instrumental four-on-the-floor experimentalism of Out Hud, a band transplanted from Sacramento, California, to the ESG-inspired Liars, fronted by Australian-born Angus Andrew. Simon Reynolds would describe Liars' 2002 debut *They Threw Us All in a Trench and Stuck a Monument on Top* as "a bit like Gang of Four's *Entertainment!* played with a Birthday Party-like looseness … less anally clenched than Go4, more Butthole-surfing."[29]

Half a year before the *Muzik* feature, Andy Greenwald had reported in *Spin* on the music scene emerging in Brooklyn. While he wrote about the variety of music that was being made, he specifically focused on what he calls the "body-movin' vanguard, mixing guitars, electronics, and shouted vocals," a category in which he included Radio 4, The Rapture, Yeah Yeah Yeahs, Liars, !!! (pronounced "chk, chk, chk"), and Le Tigre.[30] He evokes a sense of Brooklyn on the cusp of gentrification with its vintage clothing and record stores and warehouse-cum-concert-venues like Northsix, but also a picture of a close-knit artistic community. The artists he interviews explain how former mayor Rudy Giuliani used antiquated New York cabaret laws to target and ultimately shut down the underground scene in Manhattan, pushing them into Williamsburg, a historic enclave for Latino populations from Puerto Rico and the Dominican Republic and Hasidic Jews.

In framing the revival of a dance-punk aesthetic, Greenwald specifically references the "postpunk crowd of 20 years ago—Talking Heads, Liquid Liquid, Gang of Four" and the spate of contemporary reissues (e.g., ESG) and compilations (e.g., *Disco Not Disco, In the Beginning There Was Rhythm*) that showcased that particular scene.[31] At the time, James Murphy, who had moved to New York from New Jersey ten years earlier, told him, "Music stopped rockin' in the late '90s. Everyone has felt the burden of brainy, chin-scratching, boring music. Our sound is definitely a backlash."[32]

Murphy—the former indie punk, self-taught sound engineer, and cofounder of Death From Above (DFA) Records, alongside former member of British trip-hop outfit UNKLE, Tim Goldsworthy, and ex-event promoter Jonathan Galkin—soon became a figurehead for the dance-punk revival. Murphy spent his pre-teen and teen years recording music by himself on a four-track recorder and interning at former PiL drummer Martin Atkins's record label in the 1980s before moving to the city to attend and subsequently drop out of New York University. A self-confessed "control freak," Murphy epitomizes the indie record collector nerd, obsessing over intertextuality, cultural trivia, tastes, and sounds. These attributes would come to make him "king of the hipsters" in the 2000s, in spite of his being, and maybe partly because he was, a "chubby, schlubby studio rat on the wrong side of 30"[33] bent on reviving the legendary music scene of the late 1970s and early 1980s.

As in the earlier period of dance-punk twenty years before, much of the infrastructure for creating and maintaining the scene was bankrolled by wealthy, sometimes eccentric individuals. During the late 1990s this wealth partly came from the dot-com boom, but in the case of DFA, it came from Tyler Brodie, "[a]n NYU student of considerable means" who asked his father to purchase the building in New York's West Village that would become Plantain, which he "conceived as a recording studio, a movie production house and a record label."[34]

Journalist Gideon Yago later recounted in *Meet Me in the Bathroom* that "Giuliani caused a major shift in the look and feel of the East Village, but then you couple that with people in their early to mid-twenties making really good money in the dot-com boom and wanting to fucking party … Rich dudes with dot-com money got into the business of opening bars or starting record labels."[35] One of these venues that was key to the dance-punk story was Plant Bar, which Yago describes as a "big dot-com ecstasy electronic music hangout."[36] First opened in 1999, Plant Bar grew from the record label division of Plantain, run by Irish expats Dominique Keegan and Marcus Lambkin.

The Plantain recording studio was where Murphy and Goldsworthy got to know each other while doing production for Irish DJ David Holmes's album *Bow Down To the Exit Sign* in 1999. When Holmes returned to the UK to mix the album himself, Murphy and Goldsworthy remained friends and eventually production partners as The DFA. Both were invested in the mythology of late 1970s and early 1980s New York, but upon actually living there in the 1990s, they were deeply disappointed. Goldsworthy explains his first impressions of New York:

> We got over there expecting it to be like we're coming home to the birthplace of all the records that we loved, from the Velvet Underground to Silver Apples to Television to Public Enemy. Like, every single part of my record collection that is important, this is where it happened. This is the birthplace. But instead, we get there and it's just 'shoo bee doo doop doop doop' house. We were like, "What the fuck is going on?"[37]

Goldsworthy, who was accustomed to the relative popularity of dance music in the UK, persuaded Murphy, a reticent "failed" punk rocker, to begin attending dance clubs, precipitating his Road to Damascus moment after taking ecstasy for the first time.

Other members of the music scene were also working on changing Murphy's attitude to contemporary dance music. Marcus Lambkin told Lizzy Goodman that

> James hated dance music at the time and thought it was all C + C Music Factory and the stuff on MTV, and I was like, "Pfff, you and your punk rock." I started playing him good dance music but every time I was like, "Dude, check this out, this is the best record ever," he would say, "That's just a Can sample or Liquid Liquid." Every *single* time I would play him a record, he would play me the original track that it sampled. So it was this great education for me and for him.[38]

This kind of knowledge exchange led to Murphy DJing at Plant Bar, mixing music from across the dance and rock spectrum, ignoring the blending rules that had originated in the disco period, and securing a "cool" reputation. Journalist Rob

Sheffield remembered a time when Murphy "played Donna Summer's 'I Feel Love' into Hawkwind's 'Silver Machine' and I was like, 'Holy shit! That is some visionary shit!' Really, that sums up the whole DFA style right there, a DJ badass enough to play those two songs back-to-back, and you know what? Nobody stopped moving."[39]

Throughout second-wave dance-punk's popularity, there was a proliferation of related, often overlapping scenes, including electroclash, New Rave, nu-disco, indie dance (arguably the successor of the Madchester scene), and bloghouse. Dance-punk artists and scenesters in New York had an ambivalent relationship with electroclash, a hybrid genre that "combine[d] the extended pulsing sections of techno, house and other dance musics with the reckless energy of rock and new wave"[40] and encompassed artists like Fischerspooner, Miss Kittin, Ladytron, and Peaches. Though the participants in dance-punk often defined themselves against electroclash, at other times they expressed kinship with it, with James Murphy commenting that "[e]lectroclash and DFA had a shared idea: create the New York as it's supposed to be instead of complaining about how boring it is now."[41] Others denigrated or patronized electroclash for being too superficial and obviously ephemeral because, as David Madden notes in an article about the genre, it "emphasizes, rather than hides, the European, trashy elements of electronic dance music."[42]

One group that has been classified as both electroclash and dance-punk is Le Tigre. Disenchanted and exhausted with the riot grrrl scene she had helped create in the early 1990s, former Bikini Kill singer Kathleen Hanna moved to New York and began making electronic-based music with art student and fanzine writer Johanna Fateman and underground feminist filmmaker Sadie Benning. By their second album,

2001's *Feminist Sweepstakes*, Benning would be replaced by their roadie and visuals assistant JD Robson.

Writer and broadcaster Lucy O'Brien draws a direct line between the "taut chords and deadpan vocals" of Delta 5 and the Au Pairs, riot grrl bands like Bikini Kill and Huggy Bear, and electroclash groups like Le Tigre and Chicks On Speed.[43] In songs like "FYR," Le Tigre even made lyrical parodies of Gang of Four: "One step forward! Five steps back! One cool record in the year of rock-rap!" Le Tigre's self-titled first album, released in 1999, also built on the work of previous dance-punk artists by combining feminist and LGBTQ politics with danceable rhythms, this time not borrowed from funk but from later dance subgenres like technopop.

Popular tracks like "Deceptacon," "Hot Topic," and "What's Yr Take on Cassavetes" made shrewd points both lyrically and musically about who is permitted to enter the cultural canon and the collective values that put them there, destroying the rock-pop binary in the process. While their first two albums were released on independent label Mr. Lady, for their third and final album, *This Island*, Le Tigre signed with Strummer Recordings, a subsidiary of Universal that also later signed The Rapture.

Speaking to *Spin* in 2004, Johanna Fateman said, "There's such a stereotype of what it means to be a political band. We wanted to show that there's a full range of ways to express anger, a full range of ways to express feminism, and all these different ways to reach out to the community. It's about celebrating what you have and what you're building."[44] In the same article, the dance party element of their live shows is described: "the most crowd-pleasing aspect of Le Tigre's stage performance is their seat-of-the-pants choreography—fusing cheerleader poses, Motown spins and slides, and a few nods to slick boy-band moves."[45] Securing their place in the 2000s dance-punk canon, "Deceptacon" was given a Daft Punk-inspired makeover by The DFA, who were coming to be known as the "The Neptunes of the discopunk underground."[46]

In addition to remixing artists like Le Tigre, James Murphy and Tim Goldsworthy produced The Rapture's "House of Jealous Lovers," a single that Murphy describes as "the catalyst for everything next for DFA,"[47] which accurately captures the amount of attention the track garnered for the production duo. The Rapture, composed of vocalist/guitarist Luke Jenner, drummer Vito Roccoforte, and multi-instrumentalist Gabriel Andruzzi, originated in San Diego and had signed with Sub Pop before moving out to New York, where they were joined by Mattie Safer on bass and vocals in 1998. Roccoforte recalls that with "House of Jealous Lovers," "We were trying to make a house record with what we had as a live band."[48] In some ways, this process echoes the productive failure of A Certain Ratio. Like James Murphy, Luke Jenner also realized that dance music could be as energetic as punk and provide an equally communal scene.[49]

DFA released "House of Jealous Lovers" in 2002 to high acclaim. Its persistent cowbell reinforces Jenner's rasping repetition of the song title as the main lyric while the guitar style recalls the jagged chords of Gang of Four's "Return the Gift." DFA would go on to produce and release The Rapture's debut album *Echoes* a year later, which built on the success of "House of Jealous Lovers" with Jenner's strangulated vocals conjuring early Cure and PiL over a tenacious, contained groove that felt like it was emanating from a sealed vacuum.

Watching the success of "House of Jealous Lovers" and taking notes were former Out Hud members Tyler Pope, Nic Offer, and Justin Van Der Volgen, who went on to form !!! with

Mario Andreoni, Dan Gorman, John Pugh, and Allan Wilson. As Offer reflected in 2013,

> I think when we started we were too punk. I mean, the first time we got played in a club, it was, like, "Whaaaat?" We didn't think that was going to happen at all. We started doing the sound before DFA, but they were the ones who were smart enough to know that it would work in a club. And they mixed their records to be in a club.[50]

Their shift to a more electronic, danceable sound paid off when their second album, 2004's *Louden Up Now*, was hailed as a dance-punk classic, along with their single "Me and Giuliani Down by the Schoolyard—A True Story," a pointed yet funny protest song against the New York that Rudy Giuliani and Michael Bloomberg wrought. !!! also took oblique aim at the hypocritical, amoral War on Terror in "Shitscheissemerde (Part 1)," slipping in the jokey lines as a late aside: "I've got one: What did George Bush say when he met Tony Blair?/Shit, scheisse, merde/He said you act like you care and I act like I care and we both stay rich/Stay rich as/Shit, scheissse, merde."

While DFA were producing other New York artists like Radio 4 (named after a PiL song) and The Juan Maclean, James Murphy made his first dance-punk forays on his own. Calling his project LCD Soundsystem (apparently standing for "Liquid Christmas Display" and inspired by a Christmas party in Brooklyn at which Murphy and Pat Mahoney performed Liquid Liquid covers), he used a beat box given to him by Adam Horovitz, aka Ad-Rock of the Beastie Boys, and played live drums to produce one of the defining songs of both the decade and the genre, "Losing My Edge." Over minimalist beats, Murphy half-speaks, half-rants his way through an inner monologue of a thirty-something contemplating his own ugly feelings, to borrow a term that cultural theorist Sianne Ngai used to explore the aesthetics of negative affects like envy, irritation, and paranoia.[51]

In a way, Murphy works his way through all of those feelings as he watches younger hipsters with their unlimited access to music through the Internet overtake him with their "little jackets and borrowed nostalgia for the unremembered eighties." Aged thirty-two at the time of writing the song, Murphy knows he's being ridiculous, but he can't help himself as he proclaims, "I was there" at all of the major indie music snob's touchstone events: the first Can show, the first Suicide practice, hanging out with Larry Levan at the Paradise Garage, dancing to the Balearic beats in Ibiza. The song is compelling because it touches a nerve in the culture of the time and listeners recognize themselves in the lyrics.

After dropping two more singles, "Yeah" and "Give It Up," Murphy finally released LCD Soundsystem's self-titled debut in 2005, which included the previous singles and b-sides. Lead track "Daft Punk Is Playing at My House" is all dirty syncopation and clinical beats as Murphy teases each phrase out to a snapped end like a slingshot: "I'll show you the ropes kid, show you the ropes … seh/I bought 15 cases for my house, my house … seh/All the furniture is in the garage … juh." It's a mischievous, ludicrous thought experiment about bringing the French electrohouse duo to smalltown America to play a house party with Murphy's strutting, preening, slightly unhinged Mark E. Smith-inspired persona loving every minute of it. Other songs on the album like "Movement," "Tribulations," and "On Repeat" paint a picture of failure, belatedness, and a preoccupation with the process of coming undone in an effort to break from the strictures of self-righteous punk and indie rock across a fusion of Suicide, The Normal, Liquid Liquid, and Can. It's a record that both doesn't care what you think of it but also secretly cares very much.

Speaking to *Spin* in a 2005 feature in their Next Big Things issue, James Murphy remarked,

> We've been associated with everything. The New York rock scene, electroclash, punk funk. And this record has a chance to do okay. But I have greater potential as a producer, where I don't have to be on tour or be 24. I'm 35 and married. When I was a teenager I thought I was gonna be a rock star. Thank God it didn't happen, or I would have been an insufferable ass. I'm happy now because I failed—it really saved my life.[52]

Of course, Murphy changed his mind and formed a band so that he could tour as LCD Soundsystem, featuring Nancy Whang on keyboards and synthesizer, Pat Mahoney on drums, Phil Mossman on guitar, and Tyler Pope, originally from Out Hud and !!!, on bass and keyboards. With Murphy writing 95 percent of LCD Soundsystem's material,[53] other musicians have been flexible over the life of the band, sometimes also including Matt Thornley, Al Doyle, and Gavilán Rayna Russom. In contrast with Gang of Four and Au Pairs, LCD Soundsystem is largely a one-man show, with Murphy viewing most rock bands as "phony democracies" and dispensing with the frustration of interpersonal politics by writing, recording, and producing LCD Soundsystem music by himself.

Released two years after the debut, LCD Soundsystem's sophomore full-length, *Sound of Silver*, is often regarded as a masterpiece of the decade with its mixture of ironic cool and throat-catching nostalgia. In his book for the 33 1/3 series, Ryan Leas asserts passionately and hyperbolically that *Sound of Silver* is "one of the great New York albums of this century, and probably ever."[54] He goes on: "In terms of pop music, it is one of the finest encapsulations of all the paradoxes and contradictions that those of us who came of age in this century have adopted as lingua franca in our young lives."[55] Chasing the magical build of Joy Division's "Transmission" as well as the sentiment of Dinosaur L's "#5 Go Bang!" on "All My Friends" and playing snotty American on the Pete Shelley-"Homosapien"-aping "North American Scum," Murphy's bittersweet paradoxes are myriad: love/hate relationships with nostalgia and hipness, mortality and youth, competition and failure, reproduction and originality, control and release, pettiness and magnanimity, individualism and camaraderie, monotony and soar, myth and reality. These are the dialectics of second-wave dance-punk, a time when ugly feelings are the engine that drives neoliberal productivity.

LCD Soundsystem would then release *This Is Happening* in 2010, with James Murphy loudly proclaiming that this would be the last LCD Soundsystem album. By this time, LCD Soundsystem had become not only the defining band of 2000s dance-punk but one of the defining bands of the decade, especially for the cool kids. In an exchange across the years, LCD Soundsystem answered Gang of Four's "The problem of leisure/What to do for pleasure?" with "Go and dance yourself clean, yeah/You're blowing Marxism to pieces."

"Why Can't You Be More European?": Second-Wave Dance-Punk in the UK

In the UK, where DFA artists would be lauded relatively early, a parallel world of dance-punk was forming. Technically, one British group preceded and had a major influence on the Brooklyn dance-punk scene. Gramme, featuring Sam Lynham (vocals), Luke Hannam (bass), Leo Taylor (drums), and Dave

Bateman (guitar/keys), first signed to musician and designer Trevor Jackson's Output Recordings label in 1994. (Output would eventually corelease DFA music in Europe.) After one seven-inch single in 1997, they released their *Pre-Release* EP in 1999, a collection of songs with fuzzy, noisy rhythms and groovy minimalism that clearly referenced first-wave dance-punk. With its shouty scatting, driving bass, and desiccated drums, "Like U" became an underground touchstone for musicians like James Murphy, inspiring both DFA and British indietronica bands like Hot Chip. Unfortunately, they disappeared as abruptly as they appeared to emerge, dropping out of the public eye by 2000.

Meanwhile, in Glasgow, Optimo (also known as Optimo Espacio or "Optimum Space"), a club night named after Liquid Liquid's third EP, was started in 1997 by DJs Keith McIvor (aka JD Twitch) and Jonnie Wilkes (JG Wilkes) with a style that "merged just about any genre of music as long as it was good, but still with the discipline and dance-ability of a good techno set."[56] Listening to Optimo's compilations and mixes, you can tell that they were equally in thrall to first-wave dance-punk as to the avant-garde electronic music of Mute Records (e.g., Fad Gadget, Liaisons Dangereuses), New York artists such as Silver Apples and Arthur Russell, and the Neue Deutsche Welle (e.g., Rheingold, Grauzone). Optimo became one of the first club nights to play "House of Jealous Lovers" and "Losing My Edge,"[57] and hosted live gigs in addition to DJ sets. In a similar vein as the New York clubs that began mixing dance and rock genres, Optimo was developed in jaded reaction to the more purist techno scene.

Also formed in Glasgow, four-piece Franz Ferdinand eventually performed at Optimo and became one of the most recognized acts of the dance-punk genre, though their influences came from slightly more tangential 1980s post-punk like Fire Engines and Josef K. Like James Murphy, frontman Alex Kapranos had spent much of the 1990s in indie bands that remained firmly underground, and as manager of music venue 13th Note, watched from the sidelines as the bands he promoted—Belle and Sebastian, Mogwai, and the Delgados—had more success. Once he formed Franz Ferdinand with guitarist Nick McCarthy, drummer Paul Thomson, and bassist Bob Hardy, they famously decided that they wanted to "make records that girls can dance to."

Released in 2004, Franz Ferdinand's self-titled debut album was hyped as "a cracking collection of waggish new wave and angular pop (the Strokes with better belts and beats)"[58] and won the Mercury Prize that year. Journalist Imran Ahmed observes that Franz Ferdinand "took their cue from the Strokes and LCD and became the UK arm of that NYC/DFA ethos. Guitar music you could dance to. It made the whole scene so much more fun than it had been in years."[59]

Franz Ferdinand's lyrics were tongue-in-cheek vignettes of cheeky lust and flirting against backdrops that ranged from dance floors to holidays to the dark of a matinée. Facetiously named after the assassinated Austro-Hungarian archduke that instigated the First World War, they wantonly threw German into their songs, calling one of their songs about being flummoxed and betrayed by a dead-on attraction "Auf Achse" and proclaiming on "Darts of Pleasure," "*Ich heiße Superfantastisch! Ich trinke Schampus mit Lachsfisch!*" (translation: "My name is super fantastic! I'm drinking champagne with salmon!"). Kapranos's deep, plummy vocals screamed "arch" as the spindly stabs of guitar and bass pumped like pistons behind him.

With their strong visual aesthetic, including album art and music videos that referenced Constructivist art, much of the focus in early interviews and stories about Franz Ferdinand seemed to be on the way they looked. Presumably it was easy to draw comparisons between angular music, geometric cover art, sharp trousers, and pointy shoes. Sometimes pitted against the lumpen American male who wore flannel shirts and jeans, Franz Ferdinand became known as "dance-rock dandies"[60] with a queer charge: "They're arty Scottish hipsters who refer to themselves as a 'wee gang' and write songs about horny boys cavorting in dance clubs. You'd think they'd be about as popular in the American-rock locker room as the cast of *Queer Eye*. But with their surprise radio hit 'Take Me Out,' Franz Ferdinand dare to charm the backward-baseball-cap masses."[61]

This preoccupation was taken to an absurd degree when Morrissey proclaimed, "Franz Ferdinand have that 'it.' Physically they're all the same height so their eyes are always meeting each other, and they seem to be the same weight and so they look fantastic stood together. I think all groups should be like that."[62] Due to this impression of aesthetically pleasing surfaces, sometimes their music was also found wanting in depth. David Wilkinson expresses this feeling of superficiality in observing, "Bands like Franz Ferdinand were celebrated for appearing 'clever,' without much indication of what this cleverness consisted of."[63] He goes on to compare this urban artiness with the speculative regeneration of the New Labour boom years.

While I agree that Franz Ferdinand and several of the other dance-punk bands of the period may have been witty without making a comment on any of the Critical Theory and -isms of first-wave dance-punk, it was never their aim to do so. Their calculated geometry of cross-hairs, axes, and darts left behind the "academic factory" of bands like Gang of Four in favor of the humor and playfulness inherited from the quirkier, sometimes charming, end of the Scottish post-punk spectrum (i.e., Josef K, Orange Juice, Fire Engines), as well as the melody and narrative specificity of Britpop forebears like Pulp. There's no doubt Franz Ferdinand were being artful about being arty, playing up to the stereotype of fey British eccentricity through which a pronounced accent and esoteric turn of phrase automatically grant sophistication. Their darts of pleasure weren't that far off the mark from ABC's "Poison Arrow."

Franz Ferdinand encountered untrammeled success as they toured the world at a breakneck pace from 2004 to 2006, putting out their second album, *You Could Have It So Much Better*, only a year after their first. As the title suggests, they were no less ironic or mischievous on songs like "The Fallen," "Do You Want To," and the title track. On this record, they lampooned their own success and perceived superficiality, cheerfully singing, "Oh, when I woke up tonight, I said I'm/Going to make somebody love me … Well, here we are at the Transmission party/I love your friends, they're all so arty."

During their first year of acclaim and ascension, Franz Ferdinand would also receive a demo CD from an English band to whom they granted an opening slot at one of their shows. Although East London in the early 2000s was dominated by grime, out of this historically working-class area and future target of massive gentrification in the name of the "flat white economy"[64] came Bloc Party, who, despite being touted as the next Franz Ferdinand, turned out to be much the opposite.

Comprising Kele Okereke on vocals and guitar, Russell Lissack on guitar, Gordon Moakes on bass, and Matt Tong on drums, Bloc Party were reticent where Franz Ferdinand were loquacious, oblique instead of playful, introspective rather than eager to please. Their debut album *Silent Alarm* was described in reviews at the time as "about desperation, about being desperately angry at injustice, about being desperately confused with the world, about being desperately in love"[65] with "four-to-the-floor numbers [that] have an addictive momentum."[66] Their songs "Helicopter," "Banquet," and "Like Eating Glass" are both soaring and fractious, the rhythm crisp, syncopated, and tight. During the verses of album opener "Like Eating Glass," Matt Tong's drumming skitters about, imitating the stuttering beats of drum and bass, while Russell Lissack's guitar builds a churning wall of relentless oscillation. Kele Okereke's vocals, unlike others in the second-wave dance-punk moment, are more plaintive than barking.

Inspired by diverse sources like hip-hop, grime, Adam and the Ants, Britpop, the American indie rock underground, and the post-rock of Mogwai and Godspeed You! Black Emperor, Bloc Party were still inevitably lumped into the 2000s post-punk revival. They used to insist that they were more influenced by Delta 5 than the more often cited Gang of Four, which makes sense in terms of their pursuit of a more gender-fluid and sexually nuanced stance. Reviewers also noted sonic differences between Bloc Party and Gang of Four due to the different dance genre influences: "Gang of Four's jerky rhythms were once confusing, but the lens of hip-hop and drum 'n' bass has made Bloc Party's similar syncopations a lot easier to compute; their four-on-the-floor snare-drum-and-high-hat sections evoke the hands-in-the-air rushes of house music."[67]

Following the surprising success of Franz Ferdinand in the United States, which included a win at the MTV Video Music Awards and a performance at the Grammys, the music press was clamoring to place Bloc Party into the same mold. *Spin*'s "ones to watch" in British rock hyped them as "London's answer to the Rapture, with no cowbell and more power-pop punch."[68] However, Bloc Party were also often portrayed as too sullen, intelligent, and difficult in interviews, including a notably irritated *Guardian* piece by

Alex Petridis.[69] At the same time, as Petridis's piece reveals, some of their reluctance to capitulate to the press had to do with an unease and frustration with the way they were perceived as a more multi-racial, and in Okereke's case, more sexually ambiguous, band than the predominantly white, heterosexual music world they inhabited. Had Bloc Party first emerged a decade later, when postracialism was beginning to be questioned, it is likely they might have been heard differently.

The Other Death From Above: The Hardcore End of Dance-Punk

On the opposite end of the spectrum from the dance-punk bands who provided minimal, post-punk grooves, are a group of bands that came more directly from hardcore punk. Initially signed to their hometown label Dischord, Washington, DC, band Q And Not U moved into a lighter, more danceable direction by their second album, *Different Damage*, which has been described as a "combination of LCD Soundsystem and the Yeah Yeah Yeahs while staying true to traditional Dischord-esque punk, like Minor Threat."[70]

London-based Test Icicles, who as their name implies were received as "aggressively masculine in an adolescent way,"[71] was formed in 2004 by Rory Attwell and Sam Mehran, who were later joined by Devonté (Dev) Hynes. While songs like "Your Biggest Mistake" and "Catch It" seem too thrashy to be defined as dance-punk, tracks like "Pull the Lever" and "Circle Square Triangle" highlight the bassline, and thus a prominent groove, in a more deliberate way. While Test Icicles was short-lived, Hynes went on to make arguably more interesting music under his indie folk project Lightspeed Champion and his inventive R&B moniker Blood Orange.

Also coming from a post-hardcore background, Toronto duo Sebastien Grainger and Jesse F. Keeler decided to form Death From Above 1979 (the 1979 added and subtracted over time due to initial issues with having the same name as DFA Records) in 2001. Keeler "had been a hardcore kid in the '90s but was as much a fan of Midwest house and techno legends … much to the confusion of his punk friends."[72] Dissimilar to the minimal, groovy dance-punk of fellow Canadian bands like controller.controller and Hot Hot Heat, their 2004 debut, *You're a Woman, I'm a Machine*, is often deafeningly frenetic and screamy, more suitable to headbanging than getting down.

As in the case of Test Icicles, there are several Death From Above tracks that provide jagged syncopation and lend themselves to a more danceable rhythm, such as "Romantic Rights," "Black History Month," "Sexy Life," and "Blood On Our Hands." With Keeler's bass and Grainger's drums as the main sources of their intense sound, they redraw the lines of minimalism. In the documentary, *Life After Death From Above 1979*, Grainger notes that there really isn't a frontperson for the band, that he and Keeler are equally important, echoing the equal arrangement of Gang of Four. After breaking up acrimoniously in 2006, Keeler teamed up with producer Al-P to form bloghouse duo MSTRKRFT. In the same year of the band's dissolution, Brazilian New Rave band CSS released "Let's Make Love and Listen to Death From Above," in which they visually reference the elephant-masked cover of Death From Above's first album in their music video, indicating that a slightly different scene was rising.

New Rave and Bloghouse

Just as there was crosstown traffic in the earlier days of dance-punk, there was mutual, perhaps incestuous, exchange between the dance-punk bands of the 2000s, with Death From Above 1979 covering Bloc Party's "Luno," LCD Soundsystem and Franz Ferdinand covering each other, and DFA's aforementioned remix of Le Tigre's "Deceptacon." By 2005, *Spin*'s forty best albums of the year tellingly included Bloc Party's *Silent Alarm*, LCD Soundsystem's eponymous debut, and Franz Ferdinand's *You Could Have It So Much Better* in the top ten. However, by 2006, music writers were celebrating newer genres like new rave (represented by Klaxons, Shitdisco, Simian Mobile Disco, New Young Pony Club, and Hot Chip[73]) while claiming that dance-punk bands such as The Rapture were "godfathers of new rave" and including other dance-punk artists (i.e., Bloc Party) within the new rave category,[74] showing how porous the boundaries were.

In his 2006 *NME* article, "This Is New Rave," Tony Naylor appears to subsume electroclash, dance-punk, indie dance, and what became known as bloghouse under the new rave name;[75] perhaps this conflation is unsurprising as he was the same writer to announce the disco-punk scene in *Muzik* three years earlier. Bloghouse, like dance-punk, is a retroactively applied genre label that included disparate artists from record labels such as Ed Banger (Justice, SebastiAn, Uffie), Modular (Cut Copy, The Presets, Van She), and Kitsuné (Digitalism, Simian Mobile Disco) and could sometimes be known as fidget and apparel electro.[76] Common remixers of the bloghouse genre were Erol Alkan, Fred Falke, Boys Noize, Soulwax, and A-Trak.

In her history of the bloghouse scene, Lina Abascal defines the genre as being less about a similar or cohesive sound and more about "how you found it: on passion-project MP3 blogs, aggregators like the *Hype Machine*, or auto-playing from obsessively-curated MySpace pages."[77] During this mid- to late 2000s period, MP3 blogs had become a digital hybrid space that accommodated the fervor of fanzines, a grassroots music criticism, and sometimes the bland hype of the press release. Because MP3 blogs relied on the posting of free MP3 downloads, they also acted as a curated Napster and a virtual dance floor to test the popularity and reception of new tracks and remixes.

Another common feature of bloghouse was the low bitrate (128 Kbps), which could easily be circulated through MP3 blogs, endlessly remixed by artists in the scene, and played by DJs using the new Serato Scratch Live software that made it both possible to play and mix digital tracks rather than vinyl. The shoddy sound quality matched the visual aesthetic that favored the look of Polaroids posted to photoblog *LastNightsParty*.

While dance-punk was often quite carefully crafted, bloghouse was slapdash, messy, and less concerned with longevity. Nevertheless, the lines between dance-punk and bloghouse were less than solid, with bloghouse club nights like Dim Mak Tuesdays, Blow Up, and Trash hosting performances by dance-punk bands like Bloc Party, LCD Soundsystem, and The Rapture, and bloghouse record labels like Modular including dance-punk, such as Bloc Party, Death From Above 1979, and Franz Ferdinand, in their *Leave Them All Behind* compilations.

Resurrections, Returns, Retreats

In the midst of the dance-punk revival, Gang of Four reunited for a tour in 2005, after which Hugo Burnham and Dave Allen departed for good. Then, in 2011, Gang of Four released

Content, their seventh studio album and the last to feature Jon King, who moved on to run a film and content division of *Vice*, that early bastion of hipsterdom. Gang of Four used the crowdfunding platform PledgeMusic to finance *Content*, which allowed them to sell incentives to their fans at various price tiers. These incentives ranged from typical signed album bundles to a helicopter ride with the band from Glastonbury Festival to London, to, at the highest price (£1,500), getting Andy Gill to mix one of your tracks.

Undoubtedly a commentary on capitalism, they also offered an *Ultimate Content Can* that came with vials of the band members' own blood. Embedded in this move was the question of what music is worth now that it was a digital file.[78] Just as Gang of Four had created art within the paradoxes of the late-twentieth-century major label system, they managed to continue the contradictions within the context of the early-twenty-first-century music economy.

Meanwhile, in 2005, Luke Hannam of Gramme would eventually release an album of leftfield dance-punk called *Cassette* under the name Tall Blonde on Gramme's old label Output. Though Gramme's new lease on life would actually begin in 2013 when they surprised the music world with a debut album, *Fascination*, more than a decade after their first EP and a couple of years after the second wave of dance-punk had ebbed.

After five years apart, Sebastien Grainger and Jesse Keeler reunited Death From Above 1979 to play Coachella in 2011. Just prior to this highly anticipated return, they played a "secret" show at South by Southwest, prompting clamoring fans to break through the barriers and the police to shut them down early. And in the same year that Death From Above 1979 entered their second, happier life, LCD Soundsystem came to a spectacular and self-conscious end at their farewell show at Madison Square Garden, selecting dance-punk predecessors Liquid Liquid to open for them. In the subsequent years, James Murphy continued DJing, collaborated with filmmaker Noah Baumbach (including on the hipster-satirizing *While We're Young*), produced Arcade Fire's most dance-influenced record *Reflektor*, and opened a wine bar in Williamsburg.

At the time, it definitely felt like an end to the dance-punk era. Bands like Liars had diverged into a more experimental, meditative rock direction, while Bloc Party launched into electronic dance on their 2008 album *Intimacy*, foreshadowing the direction frontman Kele Okereke would take in his solo albums. !!!, too, continued to develop a more electronic sound, releasing seven more albums after *Louden Up Now*, while losing founding members Justin Vandervolgen and Tyler Pope by 2007. After touring their third album, *This Island*, Le Tigre decided to take a hiatus in 2007, later revealing that this indefinite break was largely due to Kathleen Hanna's diagnosis with Lyme disease. Other bands like Radio 4 and The Rapture had broken up by the end of the decade, while Optimo club nights ceased operations in 2010. After Tim Goldsworthy's acrimonious departure from DFA in 2010, the label continued to put out records across the electronic dance spectrum, but few were really dance-punk anymore.

When LCD Soundsystem decided to come back in 2015, fewer than five years after their fanfared farewell, it was with a mixture of "sorry, not sorry" and a self-conscious written rationale as to why, which suited Murphy's old hipster persona down to the ground.

4 Dry Drums and Angular Guitars, Rhythm and Paranoia: Dance-Punk as Genre

Surveying the dance-punk genre across its first and second waves, it becomes apparent that it exists on a spectrum rather than conforming to a strict set of stylistic characteristics. Categorization becomes increasingly difficult as some bands profess to adhere to a punk "attitude" while making music that is more rooted in electronic dance styles. Of course, as a subgenre of post-punk, dance-punk shares some of its features, which Mimi Haddon identifies as "dour (male) vocals with erudite or self-conscious lyrics, accompanied by metallic-sounding, distorted electric guitars playing texturally, not melodically; an accelerated disco beat or dance groove; a melodic bass line; and echoing sound effects borrowed from dub-reggae."[1]

In this chapter I want to explore various aspects of dance-punk that place the genre in both modernist and postmodernist contexts: (1) space and minimalism, (2) angular guitars, (3) prominent groove and syncopation, (4) dryness, and (5) literary and/or ironic lyrics. Though these qualities are not necessarily common to all dance-punk artists or dance-punk songs, I see them as integral to the way dance-punk is valued and perceived, especially in relation to its parent genres of dance, punk, and post-punk. A number of these attributes relate to principles of innovation, intellectualism, and appropriation embedded in Western modernist art of the early twentieth century, as well as associated values of rationalism, intellect, and control. At the same time, when dance-punk artists break with these implied values, they are potentially read differently or in contrast. For example, when bands like Liquid Liquid, ESG, and Talking Heads used reverb (i.e., "wetter" sounds), their music was taken to be more emotional and/or "primitive" than cerebral.

Though much of dance-punk evokes a sense of modernism, it also contains features of postmodernism that signify an attempt to negotiate the tension of the Cartesian, or mind-body, split represented by dance and rock music. These attributes, in turn, inform how dance-punk is perceived against or as a part of racialized, gendered, and classed "others," which will be explored in further detail in Chapter 5.

minimalism, n.

The practice of using the minimum means necessary to achieve a desired result, esp. in literature, design, etc.

Art. *(a)* A style of painting associated with the Russian-American artist John Graham (1881–1961), characterized by an attempt to reduce the art form to its most basic elements. *(b)* A movement in sculpture and painting originating in the mid 20th century, and characterized by the use of simple, massive forms.

Music. An avant-garde movement in music characterized by the use of very short repetitive phrases which change gradually, producing a hypnotic effect.*

* All definitions in this chapter are taken from the third edition of the *Oxford English Dictionary.*

Throughout the discourse surrounding dance-punk, you find descriptions of using space and silence, composing minimalist or economic rhythms, avoiding extensive guitar solos, and "stripping back" sound. Often, this evocation of space and stripping back is utilized to make a comparison between dance-punk and dub-reggae, which is regarded as a "subtractive" style of reggae that takes a song apart before building it back up.[2] The "minimal-is-maximal lineage"[3] that courses through dance-punk progenitors (e.g., the Velvet Underground, Krautrock, David Bowie, Roxy Music) is perceived differently from the three-chord simplicity of punk; in the former, it's seen as an intentional, artistic strategy rather than a by-product of do-it-yourself amateurism.

There are particular affective qualities and artistic values assigned to this kind of minimalism, namely, control, honesty, authenticity, artfulness, and purity. In discussing Gang of Four's "Love Like Anthrax," Andy Gill argues that the "success of the song, in part, depended on a very short and undecorated drum pattern."[4] He then goes on to tell Jim Dooley,

> I sort of see it structured like girders on a metal bridge, the things that hold the bridge together, the thing that makes it rigid—I see the drums and the bass like that …. And there are times when the guitar reinforces that and goes with that feeling of very tight structure, and there are times when it tries to sort of destroy that structure and works against it.[5]

This attention to minimalist design principles also applies to the way Franz Ferdinand see themselves, as they wrote during their guest editorship of the Style section of *The Guardian*: "Minimalists and maximalists: as a band, we tend to write from the perspective of the former, but live from the perspective of the latter."[6]

In an interview with Simon Reynolds, David Byrne discusses his use of a Fender Mustang guitar with a Gibson pickup, explaining, "I just wanted everything to sound very clean and precise, like a little well-oiled machine. I thought it would make everything transparent, all the working parts would be revealed and visible, nothing hidden in the murk of a big sound. Somehow that seemed more honest. It seemed probably more arty as well."[7]

In both examples, dance-punk takes on a quality of deliberate (read: serious) art in contrast to irrational, emotional abandon or inchoate mess. Here, minimalism means directness and systematic order. There are also connotations of purity in terms of the clean lines and abstractions of modernist art. In fact, in a *Dazed & Confused* interview, Andy Gill directly evoked minimalist art by remarking, "As Jackson Pollock is to Frank Stella, so Jimi Hendrix's 'Star Spangled Banner' is to 'Love Like Anthrax' by Gang of Four."[8] *New York Rocker* reported that ESG's sound was "so minimal (one note reverb guitar, bass, drums, congas, group-chant vocals) as to be almost pure rhythm."[9] In this pure rhythm one can hear a sonic Suprematism, "the supreme answer to nature and to the art that claimed to represent nature. Minimalism as purity and domination."[10]

Despite the constant comparison of dance-punk with dub, the use of space in dub functions differently due to its extensive use of reverb and echo effects. Simon Reynolds's comments on PiL's *Metal Box* are instructive here: "What's striking about the record is how PiL assimilated both the dread feel of roots reggae and the dub aesthetic of subtraction (stripping out instruments, using empty space), without ever resorting to obviously dubby production effects like reverb and echo."[11] For a band like Gang of Four, who sacked their first bass player for being unable to "play less," "the voids were as important as the notes."[12]

PiL and Gang of Four demonstrate how dance-punk takes the spaces and dropouts between instruments from dub but does not always refill them with the expressionistic textures of dub reverb. This difference creates a jarring, rather than enveloping, effect, stop-start instead of endless spatio-spirituality. Dooley notes that in songs like Gang of Four's "Damaged Goods," "[t]hese dub-like dropouts stand in sharp contrast to the punk notion that all musicians had to be playing full throttle at all times."[13] In doing this, dance-punk generates a "cooler" or "hipper" energy akin to the cool, sparse prose of Albert Camus and Ernest Hemingway and the "emotional emptiness" of film noir, which "traded on the hip premise that language means more than it says, and that silence communicates more than words."[14]

By using empty space, dance-punk artists imply intellectual depth as well as disruption of comfortable bourgeois linear progress, puncturing holes in the teleological myth. In second-wave dance-punk like The Rapture and LCD Soundsystem, this space, and their perhaps scholarly, calculated approach, often comes out of a Krautrock or techno sensibility, which underlines the modernist aesthetic of cool efficiency, rationality, and control, emphasizing the mind over the body, but also the more fascistic flipside of cleanliness, sterility, and purity.

Like Gang of Four, Liquid Liquid deliberately approached their music in a minimalist way, although with different processes, the former mapping structures on paper, the latter taking an organic, aleatory route. As Liquid Liquid singer Sal Principato explains, "Less is more became this recurring theme in our music and in the way we presented our music. There was a lot of open space, or unstated space, and some tracks wouldn't have structure until we went into the studio to record them."[15] In explaining how Liquid Liquid composed

"Cavern," Principato remembers how bassist Richard McGuire "thought the bass line was boring because it was only two notes. It goes to show that it's more about approach and feel and not necessarily sequence."[16]

Talking about Liquid Liquid and ESG, LCD Soundsystem drummer Pat Mahoney observes, "It's like a Chinese painting—the empty space is just as important as the notes played and the whole is greater than the sum of its parts."[17] In this metaphor, ESG and Liquid Liquid form more of an abstract gestalt in place of the intentional brokenness of other dance-punk artists. Although, this wholeness also implies nonlinearity, which is shared with the more fractured sound of their peers.

In addition to the minimalist effect of empty space, the guitars in dance-punk can also sound minimal, including through the lack of intricate solos. As with many conventional rock elements that post-punk subverted or avoided, aversion to solos could also be related to the anti-teleological nature of dance music as a genre, which forms a part of dance-punk's makeup. Rather than reaching one climax in the linear, narrative structure of rock music, often signaled by a guitar solo or a middle eight, dance music generally repeats in cycles.

In his book on Gang of Four's *Entertainment!*, Kevin Dettmar calls Andy Gill's guitar "almost ascetic."[18] Again, purity, as well as a sense of superiority through discipline and denial, is implied. Discussing the song "Not Great Men," Dettmar remarks that the guitar is "[s]o minimal, indeed, that 'minimal' hardly seems the word: for most of the song Gill bounces back and forth between two notes a half-step apart, setting off a kind of spastic siren that chimes through the song."[19] Simon Reynolds describes this guitar style as "skinny" versus "fat," which he compares to the rhythm guitar style of reggae or funk that opens up space for the bass and its melodic groove.[20] To the chagrin of musicians like Andy Gill, this minimalist guitar in dance-punk is also often described as angular.

angular, adj.

Designating a point at which two lines meet to form an angle; that forms or constitutes an angle.

Placed or directed at an angle; not vertical or horizontal; oblique, diagonal, slanting.

Having an angle or angles; having a shape or outline which incorporates or is marked by angles; not curved or rounded.

Of handwriting: not rounded, spiky.

Designating rotational motion about a point.

Of movement or action: jerky, abrupt; ungraceful, awkward.

Lacking in social graces or suavity; awkward, stiff; prickly, unaccommodating.

Of music: characterized by an irregularity or sparseness of rhythm, melody, or dynamics which is suggestive of a succession of sharp angles or abrupt turns; not progressing smoothly or predictably.

In *Rip It Up*, Simon Reynolds asserts that "[r]ather than rama-lama riffing or bluesy chords, the postpunk pantheon of guitar innovators favored angularity, a clean and brittle spikiness."[21] The angularity of dance-punk appears to have its roots in the "chucking" style of Chic's Nile Rodgers and Dr. Feelgood's Wilko Johnson. Rodgers's guitar was, in turn, based on James Brown guitarist Jimmy "Chank" Nolen,[22] tracing dance-punk angularity back through disco to the staccato style of funk.

Jon Langford of The Mekons remembers the angular sound of Gang of Four as a strategy for moving away from the average punk sound of the late 1970s: "at the time most UK punk bands were trying to emulate the Ramones, or simply attempting to play heavy metal faster. The minimalism and tension within Dr. Feelgood, particularly in the form of Wilko Johnson's trebly stabbing guitar, was [sic] a clear contrast to these musical trends."[23] Lucy O'Brien compares the music of Gang of Four and Delta 5 to the "stark campus architecture" of Leeds University, where both bands were a part of the Fine Art department, observing, "There was a similar angular, repetitive geometry in their guitar lines and chanting choruses."[24]

These allusions to minimalism, tension, and brutalist architecture again point to a modernist aesthetic, likening guitar sound to the abstract shapes, edges, and angles found in Constructivism, Suprematism, and the Bauhaus. The concept of an angle also implies a position coming from off of center (or the mainstream/predictable), bending sharply without flexibility, and rotating around a point rather than a rounded or curved organicism. The articulation of angles suggests dance movement but in a rigid manner rather than fluid, swinging upward and out from, and returning to the vertical, recalling the "traditional and classical Europeanist aesthetic perspective for the dancing body" that "is dominated and ruled by the erect spine."[25] There is also a moral connotation to verticality, in which uprightness is associated with rectitude and rational control over sexual and irrational inclinations, with the former attributes traditionally associated with males.[26] The idea of angularity conjures the avant-garde associated with be-bop jazz and its cerebral-over-visceral qualities, as with Thelonius Monk's "angular bravado."[27] With the suggestion of be-bop jazz comes the impression that angularity is cool.

This cool sound was what many dance-punk bands were aiming for, including Gang of Four, who used solid-state rather than tube (valve) amplifiers. As Jim Dooley explains, "Conventional wisdom at the time stated that tube amplifiers provided a kind of warmth, soul or humanness that was absent in the cold transistor sound … [Andy] Gill feels the idea was to get a sound that was 'spikey' and 'brittle'—the very opposite of the full and lush output most rock, and punk, bands were interested in."[28] Speaking to Simon Reynolds, Gill reiterates this point: "Valves are what every guitarist today wants—they're the prerequisite for a 'fat' rock tone, the 'warmth' that people talk about. I had transistorized amps—a more brittle, clearer sound, and colder. Gang of Four were against warmth."[29] On its own the cool spikiness of the guitar would not indicate a dance-punk aesthetic; it is the way it works with and against the groove in syncopation that sets it apart.

groove, n.

> A channel or hollow, cut by artificial means, in metal, wood, etc.; e.g. the spiral rifling of a gun, one of the air-passages leading from the wind-chest to the pipes of an organ, etc.
>
> The spiral cut in a gramophone record (earlier, in a phonograph cylinder) which forms the path for the needle.
>
> A "channel" or routine of action or life. Often in depreciatory sense: A narrow, limited, undeviating course; a "rut."
>
> in the (or a) groove. Hence groove is used to mean: a style of playing jazz or similar music, esp. one that is "swinging" or good; a time when jazz is played well; more widely,

one's predilection or favourite style, = bag n.; something excellent or very satisfying.

Andy Gill once said,

> The reason Gang of Four did well in America is exactly why Paul Weller's stuff has never done well there. Because it's the opposite of Paul Weller. I'm not being critical here, but Paul Weller's stuff, in all its guises, has never been anything to do with groove. It's always been quite jerky. Whereas Gang of Four, even at its most fractured, was always about groove.[30]

In conversation with Simon Reynolds, David Byrne discusses the shift that Talking Heads made when creating *Remain in Light*: "I was also realizing that this music that was kind of groove-based implied a whole different social and psychological thing—much more ecstatic and trance-like. I realized I couldn't think about the same things, or at least not in the same way, if I was going to be true to what the music felt like."[31]

Taken together, these two comments reveal that groove requires a certain sensibility and way of feeling. To be the opposite of "jerky," in other words fluid or smooth, and engaged in a trance-like, persistent rhythm is what enables dancing. While dance-punk like Gang of Four, Delta 5, Franz Ferdinand, and Talking Heads has a thin overlay of interlocking, sometimes competing, guitar over its bass and percussion, groove is immanent for bands like Liquid Liquid, who dispensed with guitar entirely. Writing under his pseudonym K-Punk for *FACT Magazine*, Mark Fisher describes Liquid Liquid's music as "a sound that alludes to infinity."[32] He goes on: "these grooves suspend the hectic forward motion of clock time, locking it into a [*sic*] anti-climatic [*sic*] plateau that you find yourself imagining being dilated for twenty minutes, an hour, forever ...."

Musicologist Mark Abel contends that "[g]roove music is the music of our age,"[33] defining the groove as "syncopated music with a prominent, regular beat"[34] and a "dialectical negation of abstract time."[35] Groove is usually only used in relation to what Mark Abel calls "non-art musics of the twentieth century,"[36] which excludes classical and avant-garde modernist music by composers like Debussy and Stravinsky. He conceptualizes four elements of groove: metronomic time, syncopation, "deep metricality" or multi-leveled meter, and back-beat.

In his theorization of the groove, Abel contends that what Fisher hears as an endless suspension of clock time is part of the way groove works temporally. While the time found in avant-garde modernist music aims to induce a meditative state through a deep concentration on the small details of the present moment to reach a "state of atemporal relaxation or ecstasy," groove music's attention to the present moment does not allow the listener to escape from the regularity of measured time but "rather highlights the unique significance and potential of each of the series of presents which comprise temporal continuity."[37]

In this sense, groove in dance-punk can be read as a strategy for managing and possibly freeing oneself from the metrical time of capitalism, restoring a sense of the substantive to the abstract. Put more simply, the groove, with its syncopations, introduces elements of human flexibility and unpredictability to what would otherwise feel like a mechanical process. There is also an affective dimension to the groove, which "is not to apprehend it intellectually ... rather, to understand a groove is to feel it."[38] The syncopation that is often involved in a groove provides additional potential to critique the rationality imposed by dance-punk's minimalism and angularity.

syncopation, n.

> *Grammar.* Contraction of a word by omission of one or more syllables or letters in the middle; *transferred*, a word so contracted.
>
> *Music.* *(a)* The action of beginning a note on a normally unaccented part of the bar and sustaining it into the normally accented part, so as to produce the effect of shifting back or anticipating the accent; the shifting of accent so produced. *(b)* Music characterized by a syncopated rhythm, *spec.* dance music influenced by ragtime.

Musical syncopation is based on shifting and eliding predictable accents, making its rhythms "usually easy to sing, since they often match speech better than straight rhythms [but] are more difficult than straight rhythms to sight-sing, dictate, or transcribe"[39] and pointing to a sense of orality, rather than literacy, embedded in syncopation.

In oral cultures, that is, preliterate cultures or those with worldviews still heavily influenced by knowledge transferred orally, the world is often understood in a more holistic, cyclical, or simultaneous way rather than in a linear, accumulative progression. So, it's possible that syncopation provides an experience of reality that is grounded in affect instead of reason and its attendant logocentrism, or the focus on words and language as the fundamental way to access reality. Jeremy Gilbert and Ewan Pearson propose that "[d]ance seems to resist discourse … Dance seems to occupy a critical space 'beyond the grasp of reason.'"[40]

Philosopher Catherine Clément uses the concept of *syncope*—a term normally used to describe a failure of the heart that causes one to lose consciousness or die—to critique the history of Western philosophy and its focus on mastery and certainty rather than embracing the gaps and delays in knowing. She relates syncope to seizure, orgasm, love at first sight, and hypnosis or trance, stating that "[t]here is no dance without syncope—without syncopation."[41] At the same time, she locates an interplay of attack and haven as a productive force:

> The queen of rhythm, syncope is also the mother of *dissonance*; it is the source, in short, of a harmonious and productive discord. The process allows some limping before the harmony, however: it is sometimes said that syncope "attacks" the weak beat, like an enzyme, a wildcat, or a virus; and yet the last beat is the saving one. Attack and haven, collision; a fragment of the beat disappears, and of this disappearance, rhythm is born.[42]

As with the groove, there is a bodily reaction while consciousness is periodically suppressed and the "syncope deprives the body of its obedience to the mind."[43] Clément sees the potential in the temporality of the syncope against rationality, dryness, and deceleration in Western systems of thought, writing, "[i]n the movement of syncope there is indeed a delay; but immediately, like the note in musical syncopation, this delay rushes into anticipation. The philosophical act rushes nothing; on the contrary, it curbs, it slows down, it suspends without hope of return."[44] Much of Franz Ferdinand's oeuvre is about expectation, as Alex Kapranos said in 2004: "The most enjoyable thing about songs *and* sex is the flirting … The actual point of ejaculation isn't anywhere near as thrilling as the whole buildup to it … it's more exciting to write about the suggestion that love is about to happen, being on the cusp of that passion."[45] As Delta 5 sings, "anticipation is so much better."

By observing that when "[w]e keep our reason; we face up to the little shudders and the large syncopes. We keep our heads; and so—in spite of music and affected intestines—we keep cool,"[46] Clément takes aim at the cerebral, often patriarchal, tradition of assuring a dry coolness even in the midst of the hot and sweaty dance.

dry, adj. and adv.

Destitute of or free from moisture; not wet or moist; arid; of the eyes, free from tears.

Not yielding water (or other liquid); exhausted of its supply of liquid.

spec. Of cows, sheep, etc.: Not yielding milk.

Of wines, etc.: Free from sweetness and fruity flavour.

Feeling or showing no emotion, impassive; destitute of tender feeling; wanting in sympathy or cordiality; stiff, hard, cold. In early use, chiefly: Wanting spiritual emotion or unction.

Said of a jest or sarcasm uttered in a matter-of-fact tone and without show of pleasantry, or of humour that has the air of being unconscious or unintentional; also of a person given to such humour; caustically witty; in early use, ironical.

Yielding no fruit, result, or satisfaction; barren, sterile, unfruitful, jejune.

Of persons: Miserly, stingy; reserved, uncommunicative.

Lacking adornment or embellishment, or some addition;
meagre, plain, bare; matter-of-fact.

Art. Characterized by stiff and formal outlines; lacking in
softness or mellowness; frigidly precise.

Of acoustics: lacking in warmth or resonance.

In contrast to the "energetic timbral quality" of new wave,[47] dance-punk is often considered to be "dry." Though most often referring to the deadened acoustic effect on drums, dry can connote any of the above definitions: the lack of sweetness, warmth, emotion, and softness, as well as a manner that is reserved, caustically witty, and ironic. This sonic feature, as well as its figurative connotations, is prevalent throughout dance-punk.

Simon Reynolds writes about the dry production process for Gang of Four's debut: "*Entertainment!* broke with rock-recording conventions by being extremely 'dry', in the technical sound-engineering sense of 'no reverb, drums that didn't ring' … *Entertainment!* was dry in the emotional sense too, using the scalpel of Marxist analysis to dissect the mystifications of love, 'capitalist democracy', and rock itself."[48] Similarly, Reynolds refers to A Certain Ratio as containing a "tension between dry funk (rimshot cracks and rattling snares, neurotic bass, itchy rhythm guitar) and dank atmospherics (trumpet that seemed to waft through fog, diffuse smears from a guitar so heavily-effected the instrument sounded more like a synth),"[49] while "*Remain in Light* divides into 'dry' and 'wet' sides."[50]

In the dance-punk of the 2000s, dryness was also a primary sonic quality that extended to ironic lyrics and flat vocals. This dry production quality is humorously referenced in the short documentary on DFA Records, *Too Old To Be*

New, Too New To Be Classic, in which the "disco-punk" sound of DFA is succinctly explained as "dry drums in a small room," while Matt Thornley reveals that they tape mouse pads to the drums to achieve that particular sound. Dominique Keegan notes in Lizzy Goodman's oral history, "A huge part of it was the way James and Tim engineered the drums. They were like, 'Instead of putting guitars in the foreground we're going to turn the kick up and the hi-hat and tune the drums so they sound like a disco kit.'"[51]

Reflecting back on the making of Bloc Party's *Silent Alarm*, Kele Okereke admits that their sound was undoubtedly influenced by post-punk but that the band also wanted to kick against that influence, commenting, "we wanted there to be a nod or a wink to the atmospherics and the dynamics of dance and electronic music. We didn't want it to just feel pale and grey and skinny. We wanted it to have body and life."[52] At the same time, when discussing the song "Like Eating Glass," he says, "I remember I was listening to *Marquee Moon* by Television and I really liked the sound of the guitars. That driving, dry sound. That's where I was hoping it would go."[53]

Beyond the acoustics, dance-punk is also perceived as dry in vocal delivery and lyrical style. Lucy O'Brien comments on Delta 5's Julz Sale's "dry lead vocal" and writes, "[u]sing sarcasm and playful vocals they made their lyrics deliberately dry and mundane."[54] Reynolds describes this dryness in terms of the not-quite-so-equal gender politics of the Leeds scene in which "[t]he 'unisex' brand of feminism in vogue … meant that women became tough minded, assertive, and 'dry.' The men, however, didn't have to get any more moist or androgynous,"[55] implying dryness as a naturally male attribute and perhaps that dry also connotes the more "masculine" attribution of dispassion, control, and reason.

In his 1982 lecture, "Literature as Critique of Pure Reason," literary theorist Northrop Frye opens with questions about what kinds of metaphors are applied to Western reason. In his proposed answer, he mentions light in its figurative relationship to the Enlightenment, but also mentions "dryness, often associated with coolness."[56] He muses, "The dispassionate thinker rises above the tumultuous storms and tempests of the passions into the clear air, etc…. Long ago I spoke of a popular prejudice about poets, of the type often called romantic, as based on a hazy metaphorical contrast between warm mammalians who tenderly suckle their living creations and the cold reptilian intellectuals who lay abstract eggs."[57] Seen this way, dryness is associated with unsentimentality, distance, and abstraction, not the warmth and nurturance of romantic feeling.

Dryness also drove modernists away from the subjectivity and optimism of Romanticism, with writers like T. E. Hulme and T. S. Eliot advocating for a "dry hardness."[58] This dryness is connected to a more pessimistic, limited view of what humans can achieve. Dryness is thus connected to discipline and control or the punk and Krautrock dimension of the dance-punk hybrid.

In the postmodern context, conceptual artist Sol LeWitt has called his minimal, geometric conceptual art "emotionally dry"; however, cultural theorist Sianne Ngai maintains that dryness still evokes a felt response, "'dryness' is, after all, an affective quality."[59] This felt response is related to the way a viewer must slow down to make connections between the artist's conception of ideas and what can be perceived in the art itself. This enforced distance creates gaps, or "in-betweens," that prevent easy, instant consumption by asking the viewer to step off the treadmill of 24/7 commodity and information circulation in the late capitalist world. In the words of Talking Heads, "All I want is to breathe (I'm too thin) / Won't you breathe with me? / Find a little space so we move in-between (In-between it) / And keep one step ahead of yourself."

In a way, this lag could also be interpreted in terms of the productive and interruptive syncope. Then again, emotional aridity can often be linked to the seemingly brittle inflexibility found in dance-punk's minimal, angular style, the dead dryness emphasizing an equally emotional flatness.

flat, adj., adv.

Horizontally level; without inclination.

Spread out, stretched or lying at full length (esp. on the ground).

Without curvature or projection of surface.

Painting. Without appearance of relief or projection.

Of paint, lacquer, or varnish: lustreless, dull.

Photography. Wanting in contrast.

Unrelieved by conditions or qualifications; absolute, downright, unqualified, plain; peremptory.

Of a calm: Complete, "dead."

Wanting in energy and spirit; lifeless, dull. Also, out of spirits, low, dejected, depressed.

Of drink, etc.: That has lost its flavour or sharpness; dead, insipid, stale.

Of sound, a resonant instrument, a voice: Not clear and sharp; dead, dull.

The prevailing vocal style of dance-punk seems to be either "flat affect" or "primal scream." In both cases, however, it remains "human" rather than processed or manipulated by effects like vocoder, as in some electronic dance music genres.

In a review of LCD Soundsystem's first album, Rob Young describes James Murphy's voice as "an appealing, sullen hybrid of Mark E. Smith, Shaun Ryder, PiL-era Lydon, and nasally challenged 'Malcolm' from the '70s Night Nurse ads."[60] Young's reference points for Murphy's vocals illustrate a decidedly unsingerly flatness and a drift toward a style that relates more to speaking or ranting than singing. Murphy's use of voice in many of LCD Soundsystem's tracks mimics the monotone, flattened vocals of Delta 5's "Mind Your Own Business," Gang of Four's "Love Like Anthrax," and Le Tigre's "What's Yr Take on Cassavetes?" which project a droning, repetitive quality and a lack of emotion bordering on boredom, fatigue, and depression. Like minimalism, flat affect is subtractive, having a deleterious or dampening effect on the jouissance usually associated with dance music.

The flat affect of dance-punk simultaneously signals deadness, a disengaged focus on the eternal horizon, and minimalism in its cool lack of "feminised" adornment.[61] As Fredric Jameson theorizes in *Postmodernism, or, the Cultural Logic of Late Capitalism*, flatness, or lack of depth or affect, is a recurring feature of postmodernism, which seems to push against the modernist bent already associated with many elements of dance-punk (i.e., minimalism and angularity). However, flatness was also "once a style of painting associated with High Modernism (Barnett Newman, Mark Rothko),"[62] evoking, once again, an affinity with an unnatural purity.

On the other hand, flatness can be the reaction to "equal pressures to feel too much and not enough" and signify both "emptiness and emphasis."[63] In her work on flatness in poetry, Noreen Masud, *pace* Roland Barthes, argues that flatness, rather than being a neutral absence of style, is actually a stylistic choice, in which restraint becomes a performance. The simultaneous feeling of intensity and impotence is a common combination in dance-punk as bands try to find a footing and some joy in a treadmill of competition, consumption, and information glut. This flat, neutral performance responds to the inability to see a future or imagine a reality outside of neoliberal capitalism.

Cultural theorist Lauren Berlant also relates flat affect to Sianne Ngai's "ugly feeling" of "stuplimity," which combines both shock and boredom, an overwhelmed reaction to "the machine or system, the taxonomy or vast combinatory, *of which one is a part*."[64] While Ngai uses stuplimity to analyze the aesthetic of modernist avant-garde literature, such as that of Gertrude Stein and Samuel Beckett, I think it's useful to explain the tension in dance-punk. Dance-punk combines the series of vivid presents that Mark Abel contends are emancipatory in the groove with Ngai's "extended duration of consecutive fatigues"[65] to produce a musical counterpart to the attempt but ultimate incapacity to transcend neoliberal capitalist logic.

The 2005 tour documentary *God Bless Bloc Party* shows Kele Okereke introducing "Positive Tension" with "This next piece is a song about boredom." During the subsequent interview Okereke elaborates: "I was just trying to explain the way … a group, a generation, are thinking right now about the future, about their aims and their ambitions. I think the word is *ennui*." With its stark bassline and drum pattern and jerky vocal lines, "Positive Tension" is about tedium and an inability to force change or forge a meaningful identity:

> He said, "You're just as boring as everyone else
> When you tut and you moan and you squeal and you
> squelch"

He said that you're just as boring as everyone else

Nothing ever happens

Things replace things

Days replace days

Notably, the song ends with the repeated line, "Play it cool, boy," an aptly flat response to the uselessness of getting "hysterical" about the state of the world.

Liars express a similar sentiment in "Grown Men Don't Fall in the River, Just Like That": "Everybody in his or her own life needs a hobby, fills the voids that / Work and rent, create … Not too political, nothing too clever." The maintenance of the status quo is preferable yet still meticulously crafted, as in LCD Soundsystem's "Movement": "It's like a movement / Without the bother of the meaning / It's like a discipline / Without the discipline of all of the discipline."

Boredom crops up in the context of dance-punk in several ways, from being the impetus for the genre in opposition to what had become boring about punk, indie rock, and dance music, through the propensity for horizontal repetition, to the postmodern impulse to stay interesting, and thus valuable, in late capitalist markets, even if you capitulate to Gang of Four's "sell out, maintain the interest" mantra. Interest here can be read as the never-ending need to build up enough (sub) cultural capital to stay hip and gain attention, accruing and accumulating coolness as a means to be profitable.[66] As Luke Jenner commented on the *22 Grand Pod* podcast, artists are increasingly paid in attention, not money.

Flat affect also has racial connotations: "the 'black' voice is demonstrative and communicates directly through the use of a wide variety of intonational and embellishing techniques. The 'white' voice, on the other hand, is considered restrained, gesturally restricted and *apparently* uninvolved."[67] In this formulation, vocals with flat affect are coded "white." Notably, this ironing out of affect is often paired with irony, which I discuss in further detail below.

When the vocals are not flat in dance-punk, they are also not usually read as soulful or smooth, but rather raw, harsh, and off-key, stretching and pushing beyond their capacity, and in so doing, reinstating the urgency and amateurism of the punk genre. These kinds of vocals can occur alongside flat affect in dance-punk songs, especially to ratchet up an intensity and gradual loss of control (e.g., LCD Soundsystem's "Losing My Edge," Death From Above 1979's "Romantic Rights," Joy Division's "Transmission"). These less controlled variations can also turn the vocals into a percussive effect like the yelps of Delta 5 in "You" and ESG in "Dance." Liquid Liquid stands out for this percussive use of vocals, which were supposedly influenced by Peruvian soprano Yma Sumac. As Mark Fisher observes, "Principato's vocals deploy words as rhythmic components, sonorous blocks all but evacuated of meaning."[68]

While the flat affect of dance-punk vocals can be considered abstracted, this percussive style can also be construed as abstract. This abstraction could be interpreted as "primitive" in a way that fetishizes an African or Indigenous imaginary, a prevalent trope in early twentieth-century modernism[69] and 1980s new wave by way of bands like Adam and the Ants and Bow Wow Wow. Fisher hints at such an interpretation when he writes that Liquid Liquid "delivers what Talking Heads' *Remain in Light* only hinted at: a sorcerous transformation of early eighties New York's polyglot culture into an Otherworld music that is deterritorialized in the sense that it is unearthly, rather than being blandly cosmopolitan."[70] Sal Principato describes his way of singing as a strategy for coping with the persistent intrusion of commercial interests in subjectivity:

what I consider a great vocalist is to be not someone who can sing in twelve octaves. But someone, where you hear their voice, it opens up a vista. Just the texture of their voice gives you a whole view of life. But not by what they are saying, but just how it feels … it seems life is one big billboard or one big commercial. Like everybody is trying to dictate your reality, give you this complete package of how to feel, think, look at yourself, look at others. And so I thought literal meaning should be put in the background and just the pure texture of the voice should be brought out.[71]

Having said this, Principato's vocals also bear a resemblance to John Lydon's at times in their propensity to meander and fall away. While some vocalists rely on pure feeling, or the perceived lack thereof, most dance-punk uses lyrics in what I see as a claim to both cerebral literariness and irony.

irony, n.

The expression of one's meaning by using language that normally signifies the opposite, typically for humorous or emphatic effect; *esp.* (in earlier use) the use of approbatory language to imply condemnation or contempt.

Dissimulation, pretence; esp. (and in later use only) feigned ignorance and disingenuousness of the kind employed by Socrates during philosophical discussions.

A state of affairs or an event that seems deliberately contrary to what was or might be expected; an outcome cruelly, humorously, or strangely at odds with assumptions or expectations.

In contrast to most dance genres, dance-punk is heavily reliant on lyrics, frequently in the verse-chorus or narrative structures more common to rock. For bands like Gang of Four, Delta 5, Au Pairs, Bush Tetras, James White and the Blacks, !!!, Bloc Party, LCD Soundsystem, Franz Ferdinand, The Rapture, and Le Tigre, these lyrics are invested with critical, political, humorous, and poetic meaning.

Having said that, dance-punk does deviate from this lyrical structure at its most dance-influenced, using repetitive phrases to trance-like, transcendent effect. This effect is similar to that of disco vocals, "where vocal repetition empties out language in order to open the self to divine inspiration, expressed in heightened emotive renderings of the repeated phrase."[72] This lyrical style is evident in dance-punk songs like The Rapture's "House of Jealous Lovers," LCD Soundsystem's "Sound of Silver," and ESG's "Moody." Nonetheless, this repetitive lyrical content is not of the resilient, jouissance variety as in dance genres like disco and house. Instead it implies a cynicism or calm ambivalence, such as when ESG sings, "We can go to see your baby / He can make you feel moody / Can make you feel high, feel low / Feeling, feel like, like this / Moody."

I propose that dance-punk continues to use lyrics rather than remaining instrumental like other dance genres because its artists remain "in thrall to a 'rationalist' imperative," which requires meaning or purpose above "immediate bodily pleasure."[73] This rationalist imperative reinserts the mind into the mind-body split maintained by rock and dance.

The cerebral focus of dance-punk can also veer into an interest in literature and theory. For example, Gang of Four's "Return the Gift" contains allusions to Situationist journal *Potlatch*, Marcel Mauss's "The Gift," and George Bataille's *The Accursed Shore*.[74] Jim Dooley muses on the way Gang of

Four functioned *as* Critical Theory: "Within Critical Theory, dissonance—or literally, discord—becomes a key value. Potential unity is offered by a blend of noise and melody— both point and counterpoint."[75]

Tim Lawrence sees intersections between the New York club scene of the late 1970s and early 1980s, the post-Marxist leftist school of thought that is Italian autonomism, and Critical Theory, the latter especially found within the involvement of cultural theorist Sylvère Lotringer and his journal *Semiotext(e)*.[76] Simon Reynolds also notes the productive textual exchange between post-punk musicians and music writers: "During post-punk, there was a synergy, or even symbiosis, between the criticism and the artistic practice—the people in the most interesting bands thought like critics, and indeed often were writers as much as musicians."[77]

This critical and literary trace can be found in second-wave dance-punk, too, in Le Tigre's namechecking of Gayatri Spivak, Gertrude Stein, and Eileen Myles in "Hot Topic." In an essay for the *Five Dials* literary magazine, James Murphy, who studied fiction writing at New York University, acknowledges, "My literary influences are equal to my musical influences— postwar American fiction."[78] In the same issue, Kele Okereke, who has a degree in English from King's College London, published a short story, "The Kick," about the emotional vicissitudes of a young, second-generation Nigerian immigrant on the verge of having an abortion after a failed relationship with an older man.[79] Okereke later published a story based on "Shoplifting" by The Slits as part of *Punk Fiction: An Anthology of Short Stories Inspired by Punk,* which also features a story by Dev Hynes.[80] Franz Ferdinand's Alex Kapranos published a book that combined tour diary, memoir, and food reviews based on a column he wrote for *The Guardian*.[81] It is evident that for many dance-punk artists language matters, especially in establishing depth or deflecting and coping with "ugly feelings" like paranoia.

Though Simon Reynolds has claimed that post-punk overall had an ethos of "sincerity"—writing, "earnestness was actually one of the things that attracted me to the period, in contrast to the blank, disengaged irony that's been so prevalent from the nineties onwards"[82]—the dance-punk within this period does not seem particularly sincere.

I agree with Kevin Dettmar's observation that "Gang of Four played a dangerous game by writing first-person songs and placing them in the mouths of unreliable narrators. It's a risk taken by any band, musician, or song whose mode of operation is theatrical rather than confessional; narrative rather than lyric; ironic rather than sincere."[83] The fact that Gang of Four is using a form of dance music to convey their political critique, in which they themselves are implicated and complicit, seems to be an ironic strategy. And even Reynolds wondered whether "Perhaps there was a sense deep down in which Gang of Four feared music itself—its seductive power and primal energy, its invitation to cast logic aside and surrender to mindless bliss—and all the distancing devices they used were self-protective as much as anything else, making two selves: one involved, 'inside' the music, the other detached, standing slightly outside."[84]

In contrast, !!! seemingly embrace the fear and futility of the postmodern condition in their song "There's No Fucking Rules, Dude":

Well, of course it's futile
We've known this awhile
So who gives a fuck
Let's just throw those hands up

These lyrics are both absurd and sad as they play out over an exaggerated dragging beat that emulates a sluggish resignation to dance. This kind of irony is prevalent in !!!'s music (see: "I don't look for answers, I just take my chances / I think I feel like dancing" in "When the Going Gets Tough, the Tough Gets Krazee" and "And you don't know for certain but you think you might be a bore / Don't wanna be nobody's burden so you just hit the dance floor" in "Hello? Is This Thing On?"), and it pokes fun at both the concept of "escape through dance" and the inability to summon up any other action *but* dance in the face of uncertainty and insecurity.

In an interview with journalist Richard Grabel, Laura Kennedy of Bush Tetras comments, "We're a rhythm and paranoia band,"[85] which I think is a perfect way of describing much of the irony in dance-punk. Sianne Ngai's conception of paranoia as an ugly feeling, "not as mental illness but as a species of fear based on the dysphoric apprehension of a holistic and all-encompassing system," is related to epistemology and knowledge production.[86] In other words, paranoia and suspicion are built into critical thought. However, Ngai points out that this epistemological function of paranoia "can be denied the *status* of epistemology when claimed by some subjects," meaning that the Other, whether female, queer, non-white, or lower-class, is often considered belated and delayed or devalued for their poststructural or postmodern critiques.[87]

The Rapture's debut album *Echoes* shimmers with paranoia between the taut, sparse beats, and Luke Jenner's strangled, speculating vocals on the title track, while dwelling on the same worries !!! has about being boring on "Killing": "I am the one who cannot ever see cause / I am the one who cannot help myself / Oh, you're so bored." Much of *Echoes* reflects the tense atmosphere of hypercompetitiveness and "being cooler than the cool people" that stemmed from the DFA ethos, especially James Murphy. Jenner has been open about the mental strife he experienced making *Echoes* with Murphy, who magnified the overachieving, paranoiac perfectionism in his own psyche. Though "House of Jealous Lovers" is about Jenner's parents' marital issues, lines like "one hand ties the other" could be just as applicable to the darkness lurking in Murphy's supposed idea of trust as being tied to another person by the hand while each person holds a knife in the other hand, accountability-cum-knife-fight.

In a neoliberal world where being cool and interesting often defines your value, to be a bore or less than best is to be worthless. So, this paranoia in dance-punk takes the form of a self-deprecating inner monologue. From the "nagging sense of unease without any inkling of its source"[88] of Gang of Four, to the existential dread in PiL and A Certain Ratio, to the preemptive self-critique of Le Tigre's "let me hear you depoliticize my rhyme," to the suspicious *Matrix*-like irreality of "She's Hearing Voices" by Bloc Party, to the aging anxiety of "Losing My Edge," a feeling of paranoia pulls back on the bodily pleasure of the groove while still providing a productive tension.

In October 2012, I wrote a blog post review, entitled "Planned Obsolescence and Orchestral Manoeuvres in the Dark: *Shut Up and Play the Hits* and the Story of LCD Soundsystem," about the documentary film on LCD Soundsystem's last show. In it, I focused on the tension between ironic and romantic impulses found in James Murphy's aesthetic:

> James Murphy has come to embody the anti-hipster hipster, or an aging hipster, which seems automatically to negate hipsterdom, in which novelty and youth are its defining qualities, even if the novelty is nearly always filtered through

retro lenses. Murphy and his band concept are a hipster paradox. He is ironic about pretension and knowing about his knowingness. His seemingly ironic detachment appears to come from a seen-it-all-before world weariness because he is actually older, not because he could Google everything on a phone. I think it's too easy to apply the hipster tag, which gets bandied about a fair bit; however, I'm starting to think that the dissonance I feel about LCD Soundsystem, and by extension, *Shut Up and Play the Hits*, is related to Murphy's ethos, which allows for the simultaneous existence of the romantic nostalgia of the person who thinks too much and the cynical retro of the hipster who has access to too much. He creates music infused with timelessness and faddishness, two sides of the same youth ideology.

Ryan Leas describes a similar ambiguity in writing about LCD Soundsystem:

> The binary of young experience in America in the 21st century has often been sketched out as one with irony at one pole, and earnestness at the other, with the two completely unable to coexist. Indie would either be based in affected detachment, the cool, or it would be over-the-top sincere, with an embarrassing amount of blood in every note and syllable … The battle between, and intersections of, irony and earnestness is where the issue of coolness actually becomes the most crucial in the development of LCD Soundsystem.[89]

In a way, this blurring of binaries also echoes elements of first-wave dance-punk, with Paul Morley calling the intentions of Au Pairs "political and poetical, romantic and realistic–to shatter hypocrisy and mediocrity" in 1980.[90]

I explored the irony in LCD Soundsystem further in an article, "The Irony and the Ecstasy: The Queer Aging of Pet

Shop Boys and LCD Soundsystem in Electronic Dance Music," in which I suggest that the music itself produces an irony in the performance of an older artist like James Murphy: the "repetitive and looping features of EDM, as well as its association with the alternative temporality of all-night clubbing environments, sit in contrast to the linear, teleological time represented by growing older."[91]

Like its related concept, "cool," irony is often a coping mechanism in the face of failure, which, in the case of dance-punk, can mean a failure to change the neoliberal system or a failure to succeed in such a system, placing the responsibility of success—often tied to financial achievement, but also elevation through social hierarchies and the maintenance of health and wellbeing through resilience—squarely on the individual. Journalist-turned-academic Andrew Calcutt writes, in the late twentieth century, there is "a widespread assumption that events were ultimately beyond our control; and irony came into play both as a reflection of apparently irresolvable contradictions and as a form of protection against a mounting sense of powerlessness."[92] He relates this ironic stance to "arrested development," which can be seen in the late bloomer narratives of James Murphy and Alex Kapranos. Ryan Leas views this kind of story in the context of "new millennium life" in which "many people 'start their lives' later."[93]

At the same time, this idea of arrested development and conception of failure can also be seen as a distinctly Western, urban, white, middle-class view in neoliberal times, a position from which much of dance-punk has emanated. As Kevin Dettmar observes about Gang of Four's "Ether," "King's character sings of a particularly bourgeois brand of boredom: it's only the relatively privileged subject who can view a 'heaven life style' as a trap," adding that "Natural's Not in It,"

"Damaged Goods," and "At Home He's a Tourist" exemplify "this kind of middle-class malaise."[94]

There appears to be a correlation between first-wave dance-punk's middle-class malaise and the hipster context of the second wave, in which "[p]ost-punk's complex tensions of class and education have been eerily re-animated in a social context where there's an ever-growing disconnect between the precarious lower rungs of the working class and those whose cultural and educational capital has placed them at the centre of the 'flat white economy.'"[95] Embedded in these socioeconomic formations, identity markers like race, gender, sexuality, and class greatly affect the ways in which dance-punk is created and understood. By inheriting the identity connotations of its root genres, dance-punk is inherently compromised, making it aesthetically interesting, and at times, problematic.

5 Us v. Them: Dance-Punk and the "Other"

At the crux of dance-punk's existence sits the deeply ingrained idea that dance music and rock music are incompatible or somehow opposites. This supposed opposition has been used as a way to reinvigorate and revolutionize rock, as well as authenticate, complicate, and rehabilitate dance music. In a sense, dance-punk frequently grapples with the notion of "good" and "bad" music, and within this broader dimension, that which is inside and outside, valuable and worthless, modern and primitive. Moreover, these binaries carry connotations of race, gender, sexuality, and class. In its hybridity, dance-punk often blurs these binaries, turning them into dialectics that ultimately appropriate and assimilate what is perceived as the Other, even as they synthesize.

"You Can't Be Funky If You Haven't Got a Soul": Race and Dance-Punk

As in many popular music genres, especially rock, dance-punk is dominated by middle-class, white, heterosexual cis-males. If the first-wave dance-punk artists inherited the legacy of what Lester Bangs called "the white noise supremacists" to be found in the CBGB scene in 1979,[1] the second-wave dance-punk artists grew out of and within an indie rock scene that

New Yorker writer Sasha Frere-Jones called "a paler shade of white."[2] The musicians who created dance-punk then brought the music influence of Black artists like Chic, James Brown, and King Tubby into the mix.

Of course, there is always a risk of essentializing race in discussions of what constitutes "Black" and "white" music, made more complicated by the popular music genres that have risen out of miscegenation. Mark Abel contends that "what is taken to be authentically African is itself socially constructed and mediated" and compares the Black accommodation of stereotypes in nineteenth-century minstrel shows to the narrow range of "African" characteristics adopted by funk musicians in the 1970s.[3]

That said, it is also not appropriate to ignore what is coded as particularly Black or white and what the dominant white population does with Black culture. Further complexities exist in the post-punk and new wave formations of rock, of which dance-punk is a part. As Mimi Haddon points out, "the taste community governing the new-wave field as a whole had an identifiable identity: white, predominantly male, with a positive gender and racial politics that can be read as paradoxically 'revolutionary' … and entrenched, owing to the objectification of its female participants, the niche scope of its black music inclusions, and the anxiety of contamination from the 'wrong' kinds of pop."[4]

The niche scope of Black music inclusion here means dub-reggae and disco, rather than the blues and R&B appropriated by 1960s bands like The Rolling Stones. Haddon observes that post-punk avoidance of blues-based genres and affiliation with Jamaican music, which had a more local basis within the West Indies émigré scenes of the UK, allowed post-punk artists to distance themselves from the taint of colonial appropriation of African American music.[5] Nevertheless, Haddon adds that post-punk's racial politics are complicated. Though post-punk and dub scenes cooperated politically and recreationally, post-punk's borrowing from the dub music of Black artists was a one-way street, with dub artists not borrowing musically from post-punk.[6]

In *Dub in Babylon: Understanding the Evolution and Significance of Dub Reggae in Jamaica and Britain from King Tubby to Post-Punk*, Christopher Partridge emphasizes that the history of dub is rooted in particular Black histories of resisting and surviving oppression, making it a spiritual, sacred music with religio-political meaning, which becomes "absorbed, diluted, and even emptied" in its filtration through punk and then post-punk.[7] He goes on to argue that its elements of democratic production and postmodernism may have undermined the original meaning by appealing to the avant-garde and DIY impulses of post-punk artists.

Dub becomes part of the subcultural capital of dance-punk even in its appropriated post-punk forms where second-wave dance-punk artists have consistently lauded Black music as being more progressive, future-oriented, and authentic than white music. For example, Nic Offer, then a member of Out Hud, remarks, "Our most obvious influence is probably Adrian Sherwood's On-U-Sound [record label] … Through the years we've always been influenced by hip hop. From Wu Tang Clan to the Neptunes, these people have pushed it the furthest in the last few years."[8] This comment is significantly similar to John Lydon's and David Byrne's views that disco, dub, and funk were the future in the late 1970s, and points to the "symbolism [that] recurs throughout hip: black or mixed style means new and progressive; white or segregated style, like classical music or high Episcopalianism, means old."[9]

Perhaps one of the more complicated and problematic borrowings in dance-punk was the music of James White and the Blacks, who very obviously referenced the racial connotations of becoming the "opposite" of James Brown. In January 1979 James Chance spoke to *SoHo Weekly News*, remarking, "I've always been interested in disco. I mean, disco is *disgusting*, but there's something in it that's always interested me—*monotony*. It's sort of jungle music, but whitened and perverted. On this album I'm trying to restore it to what it *could* be. Really primitive."[10] Chance later told Simon Reynolds, "I liked the idea of disco more than the actual music. I would listen to those records and find some element I liked, but I wouldn't like the whole record."[11]

This attitude toward what is largely perceived as Black music is littered with value judgments that cast blackness as disgusting, monotonous, and primitive while attempting to become a white savior paradoxically to rescue Black music from white perversion. In the same interview, Chance says,

> there was a big reaction to this disco idea. A lot of people on the rock scene were very threatened by that. A lot of people were threatened by me, by the disco idea, by the jazz idea, by the James Brown idea. The whole thing of bringing black music so upfront. To tell you the truth, some of the people were pretty racist to begin with.[12]

He goes on to defend himself from his portrayal in Lester Bangs's "The White Noise Supremacists":

> Bangs took some quotes from me for that piece, out of context, calling me a racist—which wasn't true at all. The only thing I objected to was the mystification some people put on black music, this attitude they take where it's almost like a religious thing. To me it's just music. All music has its

own technique. The Ramones couldn't play Charlie Parker, but Charlie Parker couldn't play a Ramones song.[13]

This erasure of race and reduction to technique reverberates decades later in a *Dusted Magazine* interview with Molly Schnick and Nic Offer from Out Hud. When interviewer Michael Crumsho asks them about their relationship to Black music, Offer uses Bee Gees as an example of "white guys playing black music" that "was never strange." He goes on to say, "when hip hop first hit for me, I heard [Run DMC's] *Raising Hell* and [Beastie Boys'] *Licensed to III* and that was rap music for me. You know, I knew that one group was white and the other black, but they were the kings of hip hop and didn't make any difference."[14]

Between the obvious provocations in which he engaged through the early part of his career and the later equivocating lack of self-reflexivity about his privileged position as a white, middle-class, straight man, James Chance demonstrates a complex relationship between race, embodiment, and hipness. In *Rip It Up*, Reynolds quite aptly notes that his album *"Off White"* "verged on a musical essay about racial tourism, with the track 'Almost Black' representing the most dubious homage to blackness as sexy sociopathology and virile primitivism since Norman Mailer's 1957 essay 'The White Negro.'"[15]

Music scholar Robin James contends that, "hipness emerged as a means for a certain elite portion of the white bourgeois patriarchy to affirm its privilege by rejecting what had become, by the twentieth century, feminized mainstream white bourgeois culture."[16] She goes on to argue that hipness functions with an "in-but-not-of/of-but-not-in logic." This logic, already embedded in the hipster identity as *in* but not *of* society,[17] racializes hip as "something supposedly 'of' black bodies, but not 'in' them; it is 'in' white bodies but not 'of' them."[18] By being "of" this Black embodiment, the hipster simultaneously positions himself as "of" and not "in" mainstream white culture. The multiplicity and varieties of distance in these mental gymnastics force you to contort yourself indeed.

James reasons that hip culture's engagement with the "outsider" is always about showing off an ability to "conquer or domesticate what would otherwise threaten or void one's privilege." She specifically uses the James White and the Blacks song "Almost Black (Part 1)" to illustrate her thesis, writing that the song grants authority to the privileged white hipster by noting that he is "almost black" but also "in the end … all-the-more white." James concludes that the protagonist of the song is "strongly desirable to white women because his exhibition of stereotypically black male hypersexuality is softened/domesticated by his ultimate whiteness—while hypersexuality is supposedly 'dangerous' in black men, it is exceptionally desirable in white men."[19] So, stereotypical blackness that is "of" Black male bodies turns up "in" a white male's body and is attractive. This distinction of "of but not in" runs through the tensions of the mind-body split in dance-punk, especially as it relates to the supposed Black naturalness of dancing as opposed to the awkward pathology of white rhythmic movement.

"He's Got Some Moves, but They Ain't Right": Race and Dance in Dance-Punk

As mentioned in Chapter 2, the spaces in New York where dance-punk emerged did not have a straightforward, nor always accepting, relationship with disco. Tim Lawrence asserts that a "strong anti-disco feeling ran through the Mudd Club," and quotes Mudd Club co-founder Diego Cortez as saying, "we wanted a place to dance but not to the innocuous auto-beats of the large NYC disco."[20] Speaking about his invitation to curate the *Beyond Words* graffiti show at the Mudd Club, graffiti artist Fred Braithwaite remarked, "These clubs were 95 percent white on any given night, so when you had a lot of young African American males and Puerto Ricans in the mix it just changed the dynamics—and that was a good thing."[21]

This sentiment carried through the later indie and punk rock periods, showing up in the second wave of dance-punk. As Luke Jenner of The Rapture commented, "When I first met him, James Murphy didn't like two things: he didn't like Bob Dylan, and he didn't like disco."[22] It took drugs for Murphy to lose his inhibitions and his prejudice before he became arguably the most significant proponent of 2000s dance-punk.

The other way for dance-punk artists to accommodate dancing without pharmaceutical assistance was to connect it to death and disease. Discussing PiL's "Death Disco," Simon Reynolds views the juxtaposition of death with dancing as an act of subversion and radicalism,[23] which Mimi Haddon contends is "due to the way the song bridges two opposed generic worlds: the nihilistic, angry, predominantly white world of punk, and the hedonistic, mainstream, and black and queer associations of disco."[24] In the discourse around LCD Soundsystem, existentialist mortality and hedonism create an ironic dissonance that is evident in Ryan Leas's bemused realization that Murphy's band was not the young, attractive new wave group he first envisioned: "He looked old, already. Older than expected, at the very least. He was scruffy, with perpetual stubble-beard and seemingly intentionally askew, dusty hair. Some might say he was a bit of a schlub."[25]

Mimi Haddon compares PiL's "Death Disco" to Chic's "I Want Your Love" to show that PiL's borrowing from Chic's disco rhythms and bassline, which become simplified in translation, results in "a more aggressive loop."[26] Alice Echols sees PiL's other dance-punk track, "Fodderstompf," as an ironic escape route, or "spoof of disco."[27] The irony, parody, and pastiche in relation to incorporating Black musical culture into the white contexts of dance-punk also speak to the ways cultural appropriation from non-white peoples operates as not only a method of distancing but an assimilation strategy. As dance scholar Brenda Dixon Gottschild argues,

> *APPROPRIATION leads to APPROXIMATION leads to ASSIMILATION* … What it means is that manners, behaviors, styles, trends, phrases, motifs—*tropes*—from a given cultural realm are appropriated by another culture but are obliged to go through a transformation in the process. They must be made to approximate a look and texture, feel and shape, that will meet with the aesthetic approval of the appropriating culture before they can be assimilated.[28]

Gottschild explains that this appropriation to assimilation process occurs naturally as the dominant culture continually seeks "new blood" from subaltern cultures, but these infusions must be "comfortable" enough to be absorbed into the ruling aesthetic, lest the host body rejects them. Dance-punk assimilates the Black Other by adding what is thought of as a more cerebral, rational dimension to their music. The fact that some of the terms used to describe first-wave dance-punk were "perverted disco" and "avant-funk"[29] raises additional issues of authenticity in relation to race, suggesting that whiteness has actually made disco *more* edgy and subversive than it had been with its roots in Black/Latino/queer cultures and that funk on its own is somehow more regressive or less modern than the dance-punk that replaces it.

Music critics preempt the possibility of Liquid Liquid being appropriative by reinforcing essentialist race categories and concluding that the band is actually *more* original and innovative for being white and in control. For example, writing in *The Observer*, Tim Sommer asserts, "Liquid Liquid are polyrhythmic but never *remotely* an ethnic forgery …. This restraint, this refusal to funk, makes them virtually impossible to imitate."[30] To contrast this "more 'authentic' middle-class Caucasian take"[31]—to borrow the paradoxical phrase Reynolds uses when discussing Talking Heads—is the way ESG is perceived in terms of authenticity. In Richard Grabel's previously cited piece about ESG, he insists that ESG are not "fake," opening his article: "Aesthetic theories don't hold much water in the South Bronx, which goes a way towards explaining why most of the music coming out of there is so true to life. The girls of ESG grew up and still live in a South Bronx Municipal Housing Project, the New York equivalent of a London Council Tower Block. It's a tough place."[32]

This discourse places the non-white Other in the realm of raw, anti-intellectual territory, where difference in class and race preclude self-consciousness and cerebral approaches to art. Another example of this discourse is in the articles that criticized Kele Okereke's perceived nerdiness or cerebral bent within his position as a Black man in the indie-rock-circumscribed genre of dance-punk, implying that he was overthinking and thus detracting from the energy of Bloc Party's music.

The fact that dance music was so intrinsic to the dance-punk hybrid and most often associated with Black artists, with the exception of the Teutonic influence of Krautrock, led to a sense of oddness and (dis)ease for these predominantly white performers. In Mark Fisher's words, Liquid Liquid's "take on funk … was eerie and estranging,"[33] pointing to an unnaturalness, or even sinister quality, to the white performance of Latin and Black culture.

Mimi Haddon argues that "images of mental illness and nonnormative physicality and/or resistance to systemic power—more often than not, the machinations of advanced capitalism—also appeared in critics' comments and were used to make sense of punk's borrowing from disco."[34] White dance-punk performers moving to the syncopation of Black music are seen as having "caught the disease," a neurological illness that forces them to succumb to the unfamiliar in odd gestures and contortions.[35] A very different kind of dance floor breakdown.

Part of this strangeness is the jerky, awkward dancing of artists like Ian Curtis of Joy Division, who, along with Paul Haig of Josef K, demonstrated an immobility of the waist down, implying a lack of sexuality and virility.[36] Theo Cateforis makes a similar observation about David Byrne's dancing performance, which can be read as "neurotic, paranoid, schizophrenic, and psychotic."[37] These jerky, angular movements come up again in the mechanical, piston-like stomp of Franz Ferdinand.

This nervousness as illness relates to the early modern notion that nervous conditions were not to be found in lower castes of society, who were deemed to be lacking modern, civilized attributes like self-discipline, intellect, and morality.[38] Cateforis and Haddon's observations are also rooted in the differences in aesthetic languages of dance between those of African and European lineage: "As assessed by Africanist aesthetic criteria, the Europeanist dancing body is rigid, aloof, cold, and one-dimensional. By Europeanist standards, the Africanist dancing body is vulgar, comic, uncontrolled, undisciplined, and, most of all, promiscuous."[39]

Mitchell Cohen's review of *Remain in Light* in *Creem* famously described the album as "cerebral body music,"[40] while Paul Morley saw the work of the Au Pairs as "unsafe dance music" due to its apparent "hardness" and subversive lyrical content.[41] The same implication emerges in Richard Grabel's description of Bush Tetras: "For the body, The Bush Tetras create churning, unorthodox, surprising dance music. For the mind, they disturb you with impatient railings, concise notes against hypocrisy and feverish images of love and loss."[42] This dual mind-body aspect of dance-punk, which is almost always seen as a positive attribute, continues in the second wave.

In Ryan Leas's assessment of LCD Soundsystem, "You didn't have to engage with the 'serious' side of LCD Soundsystem, but to paraphrase Murphy's own (still rockist-leaning) attitude on the matter: there was depth here in this danceable music, if you wanted it."[43] Reviewing The Rapture's second album, *Pieces of the People We Love*, Pat Long also asserts that there is a depth to their music, concluding that "there aren't enough Ibiza-playing bands that can make you both dance and worry about the state of the world."[44] These judgments are not a far cry from Phil Sutcliffe's claim that Delta 5 "have the rare capacity to be serious without being depressing."[45] This duality can also be criticized as in Barney Hoskyns's comparison of first- and second-wave dance-punk as "cerebral, bloodless, 'dance' music for junkies, the kind of posturing Gotham tripe we used to describe as 'atonal' and 'angular.'"[46]

While these white, perhaps "bloodless" appropriations of Black culture lead to a sense of unease, estrangement, irony, awkwardness, and self-deprecation, there are also borrowings flowing in the opposite direction, and the way they panned out speaks volumes about race and appropriation in dance-punk.

Although Sal Principato "wasn't that impressed" with "White Lines," he had no problem with, and even admired, other samples by rap acts and was more than happy to have Liquid Liquid play alongside the Treacherous Three in Rick Rubin's 1982 "Uptown Meets Downtown" event.[47] Talking to Tim Lawrence about "White Lines," he admitted, "I couldn't get that mad, given what a big influence Grandmaster Flash was on me … I was partly flattered, partly flabbergasted, partly confused."[48]

Liquid Liquid were ultimately grateful for the exposure and longevity granted by being sampled, but there is an awareness of the strangeness and guilt associated with contesting appropriation by the nondominant group. Richard McGuire recounts, "I used to say it was my cross to bear. It's the reverse of some black musician coming up with something and being stolen by a white performer. It's like, 'Hey, maybe I'm paying for the sins of my forefathers.'"[49]

In contrast, ESG was deeply, negatively affected by the sampling of their music. As Renée Scroggins tells Vivien Goldman, "We never had any contracts with 99 Records. It was a big financial screw-over. We were just young kids from the Bronx happy to make a record with Factory when they asked us."[50] In 1992, ESG even released a twelve-inch EP called *Sample Credits Don't Pay Our Bills*. Nonetheless, in dance-punk itself, ESG continues to be sampled, including Liars' lifting of "UFO" for "Tumbling Walls Buried Me in the Debris with ESG."

"We Got Equal Rights on Ladies Night": Gender and Sexuality in Dance-Punk

ESG also raises questions about how women are represented in the world of dance-punk. For example, Sal Principato describes ESG as having "this little squeaky sound and stuff, it was sweet. It was really sweet … we used to call it 'bubblegum funk.'"[51] This infantilization plays on both racial and gender stereotypes, typecasting ESG as unsophisticated, unthreatening, and superficial.

Just as much as the mind-body split of dance-punk highlights the racial implications of this divide, with the mind associated with whiteness and the body associated with non-whiteness, the mind side of the binary is usually gendered in favor of maleness. In her work on popular memory and cultural studies, Tara Brabazon argues that this split does not actually exist and that "[d]ancing and thinking about dance are synergetic and healing."[52] She cites feminist writers like Adrienne Rich and Jane Gallop to assert that mind-body dualism has its foundation in patriarchy, so "[f]or women … dancing is the site for commencing a revelation, a way to thrust bodies into popular memory."[53]

The "positive gender and racial politics" in Haddon's description of post-punk refer to the fact that British first-wave dance-punk bands like Gang of Four, Delta 5, and Au Pairs performed in Rock Against Racism concerts and deliberately tried to avoid macho clichés such as phallocentric guitar solos and denigration of dance music. The bands based in Leeds were particularly targeted by fascist skinheads due to a strong National Front presence in the city during the late 1970s and early 1980s. This period was also dominated by Peter Sutcliffe, the Yorkshire Ripper, who murdered thirteen women in the Leeds/Bradford area between 1976 and 1980,[54] pushing the Leeds bands toward a stronger gender politics. According to Simon Reynolds, these Leodensian bands saw plenty of overlap between the racist and sexist politics of their skinhead detractors: "Delta 5's lineup—two guys and three women, dressed in the unisex feminist style of the day—seemed to particularly offend the goon squad."[55]

While 1970s and 1980s punk and post-punk did bring more women into the sphere of rock music, they "were often seen as disturbing because they performed in a deliberately asexual way."[56] Though Au Pairs and Delta 5 "sung about or 'demystified' hitherto taboo subjects such as sex, menstruation, female masturbation, being followed home, rape, eating disorders, domestic banalities, and anxieties about physical appearances"[57] and portrayed a less stereotypical form of femaleness, there was sometimes a sense of diffidence in relation to feminism with artists of first-wave dance-punk preferring to be identified as sexless rather than stridently feminist.

When Richard Grabel tells Bush Tetras that the "frustration and anger of [their] lyrics might easily come out of a gay sensibility," Laura Kennedy responds,

> I think what you're hearing more than a gay sensibility, is a feminist one. And we're none of us radical feminists. I went through that in high school, joined all kinds of groups and movements, and got real turned off by lesbian separatists who were into moving out, owning their own farms, starting their own matriarchal society and all this bullshit. In reality you can't do anything unless you work together with people.

Pat Place adds, "Personally I think our music, our lyrics, are in a way sexless. Although I know that Cynthia has written some songs as love songs and they are definitely not gay love songs."[58]

Though Franz Ferdinand's hit single, "Michael," may have been about a homoerotic encounter on the dance floor, LGBTQ+ and gender-fluid artists are sparse within dance-punk. Some exceptions include Lesley Woods (Au Pairs), JD Samson (Le Tigre), Kele Okereke (Bloc Party), Dev Hynes (Test Icicles), and Gavilán Rayna Russom (LCD Soundsystem). One of the more visible areas in which the heterosexual bent of dance-punk showed itself was in its opposition to electroclash, which was often painted as more feminized and queer, especially through coded language of inauthenticity, pretension, and ephemerality, with pretentiousness signaling "unnaturalness" or "something faked, pretending, tampered with" and carrying a "latent homophobic charge."[59]

In many ways, electroclash was remixing the same influences that inspired 2000s dance-punk, with Le Tigre—as a female/queer band—being the only act seemingly to straddle both, while more often being referred to as electroclash. In *Meet Me in the Bathroom*, Juan Maclean remarks,

> I remember in the early days with electroclash—it was very much a Brooklyn thing in terms of its identity, and we were sitting in Manhattan at DFA consciously deciding that we really don't want to be associated. We were very aware of what electroclash was in that it was going to die and fall off the face of the earth and not have a happy death and we did not want to be associated with it.[60]

Similarly, Adam Green says, "My impression of electroclash was that it was a person singing karaoke to their own songs.

And it would rely on that person's Warhol-superstar power to make you enjoy their show."[61]

Simon Reynolds has also stated that electroclash was "style over substance," arguing that "[u]nlike earlier revivals, this eighties resurrection stubbornly resisted attempts to read anything into it in terms of resonance or broader cultural significance … electroclash's return to the eighties—synthesizers, New Romanticism's obsession with style, artifice and posing—seemed neither to be in synch with or opposed to post-millennium culture."[62] What Reynolds overlooks is the fact that electroclash did hold cultural significance for queer artists and fans. The blend of performance art and electronic music appealed *because* it played with identity and created safe spaces to do so.[63] Electroclash's sense of ludic resistance made it the foil to dance-punk, just as dance-punk was the foil to self-serious indie rock.

These negative comments about electroclash show how, within the discourse that surrounds dance-punk, authenticity and value are to be found exclusively in the ease with which a text can be "read" by a cultural critic. Whereas much of the discourse on dance-punk itself has painted the genre as a fun, less serious alternative, in his review of The Rapture's *Echoes*, *Pitchfork*'s Ryan Schreiber reveals this impulse by writing that dance-punk represented "indie rock cultivating a new loathing and defiance for tired hipster poses and demanding the chaos of which safety and careerism had stripped it."[64] With its close association with hipsterism, dance-punk is undeniably cool in relation to electroclash, which was decidedly uncool.

As shown through Susan Fraiman's book *Cool Men and the Second Sex* and the limited examples of female hipsters in *What Was the Hipster?*, "cool," like hip, irony, and knowledge production, is most often conceived of as the domain of the male. At the same time, "cool" dominates second-wave dance-punk, endlessly appearing in accounts of the period like *Meet Me in the Bathroom*.

"We're So Cool": Class, Race, and Dance-Punk

According to journalists Dick Pountain and David Robins, cool is a "*permanent* state of *private* rebellion"[65] associated with "narcissism, ironic detachment and hedonism,"[66] which also favors "a retarded adolescence, inspired in part by a morbid fear of ageing."[67] With its anti-social stance, cool is easily absorbed into the neoliberal world of late capitalism, a world where losing one's edge can feel like the end of the world.

Surveying cool as an idea, design scholar Vanessa Brown observes that cool is "implicated in the pressing questions of contemporary life—politics, identity politics, work in the so-called 'creative industries,' transition from unsustainable behaviours and consumption"[68]—despite its slipperiness as a term that can mean both authenticity and inauthenticity.[69] She identifies five overlapping themes based on the existing literature with cool as: a survival strategy of the modern world, "a mode of capitalism," a youth-driven way of gaining distinction through consumerism, a reaction to "the culture of technical rationality," and rebellion through "performances of affectlessness."[70]

She goes on to say that twenty-first-century hipsters' tastes may fuel trends, as those of the bohemians before them did, but hipsters' sense of individualism ends up being part of the neoliberal machine, turning the punk manifesto of "Do-It-Yourself" into "You're On Your Own."[71] Hipsterism is a defense mechanism in a neoliberal world increasingly in need of affective labor, which can be done for little to no financial compensation as shown earlier by Balzer's criticisms of curationism. Those with privilege, whether due to race, class, gender, or sexuality, can afford to engage in more affective labor than those without safety nets.

As discussed in several histories of cool, including Joel Dinerstein's book on postwar American cool, there is a significant and historical racial dimension to cool and hip in relation to appropriation and assimilation as a coping strategy and as a desire for (sub)cultural capital. The aspect of irony within the hipster profile, which rose in parallel with indie rock[72] and is mobilized in the "whiteness" of 2000s hipsters, can be a dangerous detachment from the meanings, accountability, power structures, and racism entrenched in the white signifiers wielded by hipsters as fashion and culture.

In his book *Decolonize Hipsters*, Grégory Pierrot explores these colonial markers in twenty-first-century hipster irony. Referring to the sartorial choices of hipsters, including Hitler Youth haircuts, trucker hats, and T-shirts with suburban or smalltown associations with parochial organizations like little league, he argues that "[t]he cliché signifiers of white working-class subculture … were worn precisely for the utter whiteness they represented, the irony resting necessarily on the very menace these signs packed."[73]

Pierrot extends his argument to the punk and post-punk music favored by late 1990s hipsters (and I would argue the dance-punk loved by early 2000s hipsters), which he asserts to be "ancestral and revered scenes, and ever-ready sources for models, sincere or ironic, known or obscure,"[74] connecting the "ironic" fascist imagery of punk and post-punk bands like Joy Division (and post-punk influences like Kraftwerk) to the menacing irony built into the white hipster persona. Notably, Pierrot problematizes the retromania of twenty-first-century hipsters not for its lack of originality and progressive novelty, but in its complete erasure of Black sources: "Latter-day hipsters and their icons could just pretend they did not need blackness at all, notably by imitating the original white imitators, and presenting that imitation as innovation."[75] It is this post-racial attitude, which flattens and disregards identity markers that continue to have real impacts on non-white lives, that absorbs racial difference and pronounces it cool.

In her book, *Way Too Cool: Selling Out Race and Ethics*, Shannon Winnubst explores the aesthetic of "coolness" in relation to the current neoliberal age, which she argues "speaks in the language of cool"[76] and has led to a "twinned erasure of race and ethics from our social lexicon."[77] Winnubst contends that individual success is fully measured and calculated in economic terms,[78] thus, the ethical language of "right and wrong" shifts to the language of "success and failure."[79] Within this context, "the more you can intensify interests, the more expansive, enterprising, and interesting you are,"[80] which relates directly to your success as a neoliberal subject.

Much like the shift to a post-racial ideology and the emptying of meaning from the Black music used in dance-punk, the neoliberal impulse to view everything in terms of economic calculation and investment flattens social difference into fungibility, or simple interchangeability.[81] So, coolness, then, becomes the tool used to swap out and transcend various differences—that ironically become the same, or at the very least perceived as equal, in this easy interchangeability—in a perpetual search for individual success.

In the midst of this coolness and fungibility, the dance side of the dance-punk hybrid becomes the way to make meaning and use out of the punk side. Appearing on the *Sound Opinions* podcast in 2010, James Murphy draws the following analogy:

> Dance music really woke me back up because, suddenly, coming from an indie rock background I was, like, what was the point? … And you realize the point of all of it was to feel cool. I mean, it's what almost everybody in the band wanted to do. They wanted to be cool, they wanted to feel cool. They wanted other people to think certain things about them. And if you took that away, what was the point? The music was boring, like, most of it was crappy, it sounded bad. The songs weren't there. Nobody could sing. It's, like, what was the point of any of it?
>
> So, dance music had a point. You could tell when it worked. It was, like, did people dance? Well, then it worked … I started equating it to like, you know, being in indie rock, making fake cakes, you know, Styrofoam. And dance music … you were cooking, you made food, like, people ate it. And if they liked it, then it was good food. But no matter what it was like, it was there for a reason. You were gonna play it and dance or not. It really struck a chord with me … a simple set of goals … within which you can make it especially delicious … There was a point, and the point wasn't art. The point was something else. And then you were free to kind of, like, do as much weird stuff as you wanted, as long as you did the basic job of making it danceable.

This utilitarian, functionalist view of dance music is not new but Murphy's comparison between the existential crisis of indie rock and the real-time impact of dance music is interesting on a few levels.

There's a sense that the exchange value of cool in indie rock is bankrupt, and indie rock is, therefore, difficult to measure in terms of success and rational use. Conversely, dance music is grounded in use value and some kind of human necessity (i.e., real food as opposed to decorative facsimiles). In a complete reversal of prevailing rock attitudes, dance music becomes the more authentic genre by virtue of its bodily impact and measurable outcomes. It's a paradoxical mix of utilitarianism and neoliberal logic. Dance-punk is the practical escape route out of the symbolic value of indie rock and perhaps the sneaking suspicion that the creative industries and the coolness they esteem are not a sound investment.

Afterword—Losing Its Edge? Whither Dance-Punk

At the time of completing this book, more than two decades on from its last incarnation, dance-punk is primarily glimpsed through retrospectives and reunion performances. LCD Soundsystem had recently performed on an episode of *Saturday Night Live*. Franz Ferdinand released their greatest hits compilation *Hits to the Head*. Bloc Party, after losing original members Matt Tong and Gordon Moakes and touring their debut *Silent Alarm* over 2018 and 2019, are poised to release a new record, *Alpha Games*. After reuniting for some shows in 2019, individual members of The Rapture continued to produce their own music with Luke Jenner's 2020 album *1* and Gabriel Andruzzi and Vito Roccoforte's records as Mother of Mars and Wah Together. Bush Tetras played a gig with Public Practice and Sunk Heaven with a live DJ set from Bill Bahlman at Le Poisson Rouge. The documentary film adaptation of Lizzy Goodman's *Meet Me in the Bathroom* premiered at Sundance.

There may no longer be an Optimo club night, but there is now a Disco Unusual club night at The Hope & Ruin in Brighton. The 2022 Ain't No Picnic Festival will be headlined by LCD Soundsystem and the Strokes, as well as feature a reunion performance from Le Tigre. Meanwhile, the hip cache of old dance-punk is being used to sell a variety of products, including iPhones (Delta 5's "Mind Your Own Business"), the

Samsung S21 Ultra (Liquid Liquid's "Cavern"), and even the Invitation to Lexus Sale Event (ESG's "Dance"). The relatively recent passing of Andy Gill and Julz Sale has begun the slow erosion of the first wave of dance-punk, though the first and second waves of dance-punk occasionally still collide as with the guest appearance of James Chance on his fractious sax for Franz Ferdinand's performance of "Feel the Love Go" on the *Late Show with Stephen Colbert* in 2018. Ever the exception, Gramme continues to work their idiosyncratic dance-punk groove with 2019's *Disco Lovers* album and their recent cool-baiting collaboration with A Certain Ratio.

In 2021, former editor of *The Vinyl Factory* Anton Spice reported on what he sees as the next phase of dance-punk in a world now dominated by Spotify and Bandcamp, rather than MySpace and *The Hype Machine*, listing artists such as MadMadMad, Tom of England, Automatic, and New Fries.[1] I would add a few more bands to this list, including British trio Shopping, who have been releasing records that strive for queer radical joy amid ubiquitous consumerism since 2013; Public Practice, the aforementioned openers for Bush Tetras who are newly engaging with the compromises of previous waves of dance-punk; and Montreal-based Pottery, who released their tongue-in-cheek debut album, *Welcome to Bobby's Motel*, in 2020. It remains to be seen whether this next wave, which exists in an even more atomized world of tastes than twenty years ago, will solidify into a scene that captures the imagination, the discourse, and the dance floor. As with related musical genres and scenes of the 2000s (e.g., bloghouse), it appears to have reemerged, sometimes under the guise of "indie sleaze."[2]

Contemporary critics were often sarcastic and patronizing about the second wave of dance-punk. In a tongue-in-cheek guide to music jargon in *The Globe and Mail*, Carl Wilson described dance-punk as "New York-based indie rock … fixated on the moment when disco-new-wave fusions left off in the early 1980s … Talking Heads still did it better."[3]

Simon Reynolds has been one of the most vocal critics of this second wave. In *Retromania*, he largely dismisses the post-punk (dance-punk) revival of the 2000s with the exception of LCD Soundsystem, whom he finds "interesting and moving, but also a timely and telling response to the present" because the band confirms that his "potential responses, as an old modernist-minded post-punk, already nag away inside Murphy's guts. Although quite a bit younger, he's someone who grew up on punk and art-rock values, who's torn between his attachment to rock's heritage and his equally powerful urge to create something completely new. The result is a volatile cocktail of rage and self-loathing."[4]

In Reynolds's view, popular music must be "new," in all its subjectivity, or it ceases to have value as a cultural text. A listener must also be a knowledge insider to perceive and judge whether a type of music is new or derivative. Murphy's former production partner, Tim Goldsworthy, largely holds a similar view. In his remarks about "Losing My Edge," he says, "Do I like that track? No, I hate it, to be honest, because I know the things that are being ripped off. 'Losing My Edge' is a direct rip-off of a Killing Joke track ['Change'] … I hate it because it's devalued those tracks."[5]

Robert Loss counters views like Reynolds in his discussion of the politics of novelty in *Nothing Has Been Done Before: Seeking the New in 21st-Century American Popular Music*, arguing that

> [f]or all of Reynolds' concern with time in *Retromania*, the irony is that his book is obsessed by form and genre, by material and discipline, without much accounting for

historical or cultural context outside of music itself ... The question still remains a matter of scale, the event as opposed to the swerve, a revolution in the cultural archive as opposed to an editing of a tradition, but a replicating, derivative sound can still be new if it makes some argument about its current moment, or if it makes some distinction between the present and the past.[6]

In the case of dance-punk there did seem to be a swerve, and perhaps sometimes it was away from the politics and aesthetics of dislocation that concerned so-called progressive artists of the late 1970s, but it was also a veering into the question of what kind of art and meaning can be made in a flatter, more temporally static world.

Another way to look at dance-punk is as a series of mistranslations and imperfect imitations that yielded a genre of music that moved people in a variety of ways, to different points of view, to sonic expression of contradiction, to catharsis, to the dancefloor. These imprecise repetitions from the late 1970s to the present created a hybrid that brought the mind and body closer together, sometimes with friction, sometimes with liberation. New angles can pop out of these repetitions with difference, including the reclamatory "performance of a performance" of Black hipsters.[7]

With its perceived combination of thinking and dancing, critiquing and escaping, perhaps dance-punk could be seen as a reaction to crisis—the first wave responding to the apparent failure of the left and the exhaustion, cynicism, and encroaching neoliberal turn of the 1980s; the second wave responding to the "end of history," the fungibility of difference, and the futile "war on terror." Despite the financial crisis of 2008, neoliberalism has only become more entrenched in a "zombie" form,[8] lumbering on in its one-track focus even though it does not make sense, especially for 99 percent of the population.

The feeling in the 2000s that everything was instantly available and that the past and future had collapsed into the present also dramatically deepened, culminating in what media theorist Douglas Rushkoff has called "present shock," where people "end up reacting to the ever-present assault of simultaneous impulses and commands,"[9] instead of being able to plan ahead or engage in sustained dialogue or deep understanding. The "Why Theory?" of Gang of Four has shifted to the *Why Choose?* of Shopping. The paranoia of the late twentieth century and early 2000s has morphed into what Rushkoff terms "fractalnoia," a state of contextless connections and links that appear to make meaning but often obfuscate real causes and complexities.[10] Now that the world is in the midst of Covid-19, the war in Ukraine, technocratic billionaires, climate change, intensifying culture wars, and the reckoning of Black Lives Matter and #MeToo, we are at yet another conjuncture of crisis and potential, which has already seemed partially to result in the "future nostalgia" of a new wave of disco.[11]

As Kele Okereke reflects in a recent interview regarding Bloc Party's new album and twenty-year career,

> I guess there are two sorts of artists right now. There are people that need a distraction from what's happening right now in the world, and I get that on some level … But there are also artists that feel that now it's time more than ever to be commenting on what's happening, because it is so frightening. And I know as artists, we do have a voice and a platform, and an opportunity to turn our anxiety into art that helps people.[12]

To me, dance-punk is obviously personal because it was one of the major musical genres soundtracking my late teens and early adulthood. In a piece commemorating the fifteenth anniversary of Bloc Party's *Silent Alarm*, Miles Raymer recalls:

> 2005 was a weird time to be going out clubbing. The news was full of war and terrorism, and living in a city meant learning to live in a heavy cloud of ambient anxiety. Dance punk offered relief from that pressure, but it was also saturated with references to it: house beats sped up to manic tempos, guitar lines reduced to jags of discordant noise, and lyrics about alienation and psychic tension.[13]

For me, dance-punk eased not only the mental unease generated by geopolitical pressures but the internal struggle I was experiencing as a seemingly directionless young adult. I was already tired of the expectations to compete and promote myself like an infinitely adaptable brand. I felt overstimulated and overwhelmed by the access to so many potential ideas and paths but also stymied in the life choices that should matter. I didn't always want to vent my frustration through angry punk, brooding indie ballads, or nihilistic industrial noise. Dance-punk was versatile enough to bridge my negative, cynical thoughts and my need to exorcise the energy from my existential crisis. It was a compromised escape, which was probably all my overthinking brain could really manage at the time.

When I was learning how to DJ roughly eight years ago, I naturally gravitated toward the James Murphy school of "play what you love without worrying about the bpm." My setlists could include music from any genre I loved, arty glam rock, Northern Soul, post-punk, Krautrock, disco, Motown, punk, synthpop, garage rock, electro-funk, and techno. They could span songs by Longpigs, Simple Minds, Algiers, Death, and Young Fathers, or from Echo and the Bunnymen through Wild Beasts and FKA Twigs to Life Without Buildings. Many of my sets drew on dance-punk artists like Bush Tetras, Au Pairs, Gang of Four, Radio 4, The Rapture, LCD Soundsystem, and Shopping. As in the early days for James Murphy, I could absolutely clear a floor by putting on certain tracks that were truly only loved by my DJ partner-in-crime Laura and me. But sometimes, I could hit upon a magic moment when people lost their minds dancing to something they'd never expected or never heard before.

10 Essential Tracks

First-Wave Dance-Punk Ten Essential Tracks

1. Public Image Ltd. "Death Disco"
2. Gang of Four "Natural's Not In It"
3. Delta 5 "Mind Your Own Business"
4. Au Pairs "We're So Cool"
5. Bush Tetras "Too Many Creeps"
6. A Certain Ratio "Shack Up"
7. James White and the Blacks "Contort Yourself (August Darnell Remix)"
8. Talking Heads "The Great Curve"
9. ESG "Moody"
10. Liquid Liquid "Cavern"

Second-Wave Dance-Punk Ten Essential Tracks

1. Le Tigre "Deceptacon"
2. The Rapture "House of Jealous Lovers"
3. !!! "Me and Giuliani Down by the Schoolyard—A True Story"
4. LCD Soundsystem "Losing My Edge"
5. Radio 4 "Dance to the Underground"
6. Bloc Party "Banquet"
7. Franz Ferdinand "Take Me Out"

8. Test Icicles "Circle Square Triangle"
9. Liars "Tumbling Walls Buried Me in the Debris with ESG"
10. Death From Above 1979 "Sexy Results"

Dance-Punk Spotify Playlist:

https://open.spotify.com/playlist/5re2KO7UQQD2oPHm3cg
UZU

Recommended Listening

!!!. *!!!*. Gold Standard, 2001.

!!! *Louden Up Now*. Touch and Go, 2004.

A Certain Ratio. "Do the Du (Casse)/Shack Up." Factory, 1981.

A Certain Ratio. *To Each*. Factory, 1981.

Au Pairs. *Playing with a Different Sex*. Human Records, 1981.

Au Pairs. *Sense and Sensuality*. Kamera Records, 1982.

Big Two Hundred. *Your Personal Filth*. D.C. Recordings, 2002.

Bloc Party. *Silent Alarm*. Wichita, 2005.

Bush Tetras. *Boom in the Night (Original Studio Recordings 1980–1983)*. ROIR, 1995.

Chemical Restraint. *Kiss Off*. Terrible Tapes, 2019.

controller.controller. *History*. Paper Bag, 2004.

controller.controller. *X-Amounts*. Paper Bag, 2006.

Death From Above 1979. *You're a Woman, I'm a Machine*. Last Gang, 2004.

Death From Above 1979. *The Physical World*. Last Gang, 2014.

Delta 5. "Mind Your Own Business/Now That You're Gone." Rough Trade, 1979.

Delta 5. "Anticipation/You." Rough Trade, 1980.

Delta 5. *See the Whirl*. PRE Records, 1981.

ESG. "You're No Good." Factory, 1981.

ESG. *Come Away with ESG*. 99, 1983.

Franz Ferdinand. *Franz Ferdinand*. Domino, 2004.

Franz Ferdinand. *You Could Have It So Much Better*. Domino, 2005.

Franz Ferdinand. *Tonight: Franz Ferdinand*. Domino, 2009.

Gang of Four. *Entertainment!* EMI, 1979.

Gang of Four. *Solid Gold*. EMI, 1981.

Gramme. *Pre-Release*. Output, 1999.

Gramme. *Fascination*. Tummy Touch, 2013.

Gramme. *Disco Lovers*. Love Vinyl, 2019.

Hot Hot Heat. *Make Up the Breakdown*. Sub Pop, 2002.

James White and the Blacks. *"Off White."* ZE, 1979.

Joy Division. "She's Lost Control." *Unknown Pleasures*, Factory, 1979.

Joy Division. "Transmission/Novelty." Factory, 1979.

LCD Soundsystem. "Losing My Edge/Beat Connection (Extended Disco Dub)." DFA, 2002.

LCD Soundsystem. *LCD Soundsystem*. DFA, 2005.

LCD Soundsystem. *Sound of Silver*. DFA, 2007.

LCD Soundsystem. *This Is Happening*. DFA, 2010.

LCD Soundsystem. *American Dream*. DFA, 2017.

Le Tigre. *Le Tigre*. Mr. Lady, 1999.

Le Tigre. *Feminist Sweepstakes*. Mr. Lady, 2001.

Le Tigre. *This Island*. Universal, 2004.

Liars. *They Threw Us All in a Trench and Stuck a Monument on Top*. Gern Blandsten Records, 2001.

Liquid Liquid. *Liquid Liquid*. 99, 1981.

Liquid Liquid. *Successive Reflexes*. 99, 1981.

Liquid Liquid. *Optimo*. 99, 1983.

Moving Units. *Moving Units*. Three One G, 2002.

Moving Units. *Dangerous Dreams*. Palm, 2004.

Out Hud. *S.T.R.E.E.T.D.A.D.* Kranky, 2002.

Pottery. *Welcome to Bobby's Motel*. PTKF/Partisan, 2020.

Public Image Ltd. "Fodderstompf." *Public Image Ltd.*, Virgin, 1978.

Public Image Ltd. "Death Disco." Virgin, 1979.

Public Image Ltd. "Memories." *Metal Box*, Virgin, 1979.

Public Practice. *Gentle Grip*. Wharf Cat Records, 2020.

Pylon. *Gyrate Plus*. DB Records, 1980.

Q And Not U. *Different Damage*. Dischord, 2002.

Q And Not U. *Power*. Dischord, 2004.

Radio 4. *Dance to the Underground*. Gern Blandsten Records, 2001.

Radio 4. *Gotham!* City Slang, 2002.

The Rapture. *Echoes*. DFA, 2003.

The Rapture. *Pieces of the People We Love*. Universal, 2006.

The Rapture. *In the Grace of Your Love*. DFA, 2011.

Section 25. "Dirty Disco." *Always Now*, Factory, 1981.

Shopping. *Consumer Complaints*. FatCat Records, 2013.

Shopping. *Why Choose*. FatCat Records, 2015.

Shopping. *The Official Body*. FatCat Records, 2018.

Shopping. *All or Nothing*. FatCat Records, 2020.

Talking Heads. *Remain in Light*. Sire, 1980.

Talking Heads. *Speaking in Tongues*. Sire, 1983.

Test Icicles. *For Screening Purposes Only*. Domino, 2005.

Tussle. *Kling Klang*. Troubleman Unlimited, 2004.

Various. *Disco Not Disco*. Strut Records, 2000.

Various. *Disco Not Disco 2*. Strut Records, 2002.

Various. *Dance to the Underground*. Muzik, 2003.

Various. *New York Noise*. Soul Jazz, 2003.

Various. *Disco Not Disco 3*. Strut Records, 2008.

The White Rose Movement. *Kick*. Craft, 2006.

Recommended Viewing

12 Years of DFA: Too Old To Be New, Too New To Be Classic. Directed by Max Joseph, Red Bull Music Academy, 2013.

Class Divide. Directed by Marc Levin, Blowback, 2015.

Downtown '81. Directed by Edo Bertoglio, New York Beat Films, 2001.

God Bless Bloc Party. Directed by Ace Norton and Charles Spano, Wichita, 2005.

Life After Death From Above 1979. Directed by Eva Michon, Last Gang, 2014.

My Brooklyn. Directed by Kelly Anderson, New Day Films, 2012.

The Public Image Is Rotten. Directed by Tabbert Fiiller, Verisimilitude, 2017.

The Punk Singer. Directed by Sini Anderson, Sundance Selects, 2013.

The Rapture Is Live, and Well, in New York City. Directed by Patrick Daughters, Vertigo, 2004.

Shut Up and Play the Hits: The Very Loud Ending of LCD Soundsystem. Directed by Will Lovelace and Dylan Southern, Pulse Films, 2012.

Urgh! A Music War. Directed by Derek Burbidge, Filmways, 1981.

Who Took the Bomp? Le Tigre on Tour. Directed by Kerthy Fix, Fix Films, 2010.

Notes

Chapter 1

1 Liam Inscoe-Jones, "Burn the Dancefloor: The Raucous History of Dance Punk," *Sorry Scholar*, February 21, 2019, https://thesorryscholar.com/2019/02/21/burn-the-dancefloor-the-raucus-history-of-dance-punk/.

2 "Dance-Punk Music Guide: 5 Notable Dance-Punk Acts," *MasterClass*, February 24, 2022, https://www.masterclass.com/articles/dance-punk-music-guide.

3 Ian King, *Appetite for Definition: An A-Z Guide to Rock Genres* (Harper, 2018), 104–5.

4 Mimi Haddon, *What Is Post-Punk? Genre and Identity in Avant-Garde Popular Music, 1977–82* (University of Michigan Press, 2020), 3.

5 Mark Neocleous, "Resisting Resilience," *Radical Philosophy* 178 (March/April 2013), 5, https://www.radicalphilosophyarchive.com/issue-files/rp178_commentary_neocleous_resisting_resilience.pdf.

6 Ryan Moore, *Sells Like Teen Spirit: Music Youth Culture and Social Crisis* (New York University Press, 2010), 15.

7 Charles Kronengold, "Exchange Theories in Disco, New Wave, and Album-Oriented Rock," *Criticism* 50, no. 1 (2008), 46.

8 Wendy Fonarow, *Empire of Dirt: The Aesthetics and Rituals of British Indie Music* (Wesleyan University Press, 2006), 72.

9   John J. Scheinbaum, *Good Music: What It Is and Who Gets to Decide* (University of Chicago Press, 2018), 124.

10   Ibid., 227.

Chapter 2

1   Peter Shapiro, *Turn the Beat Around: The Secret History of Disco* (Faber, 2005), 13.

2   Tim Lawrence, *Love Saves the Day: A History of American Dance Music Culture, 1970–1979* (Duke University Press, 2003).

3   Alice Echols, *Hot Stuff: Disco and the Remaking of American Culture* (W. W. Norton, 2010), 8–9.

4   Shapiro, *Turn the Beat Around*, 16–17.

5   Echols, *Hot Stuff*, xxv.

6   Ibid., 12.

7   Ibid., 15.

8   Ibid.

9   Ibid., 17.

10   Ibid., 21.

11   Ibid., 15–16.

12   Ibid., 16.

13   Ibid., 29.

14   Ibid.

15   Daryl Easlea, *Everybody Dance: Chic and the Politics of Disco* (Omnibus, 2020), xxvi.

16   Echols, *Hot Stuff*, 30.

17   Ibid.

18 Ibid., 53.

19 Richard Dyer, "In Defence of Disco," *Gay Left*, no. 8 (1979), 23.

20 Ibid.

21 Echols, *Hot Stuff*, 74.

22 Ibid., 23.

23 Ibid., 75.

24 Dyer, "In Defence," 22.

25 Echols, *Hot Stuff*, 112.

26 Ibid., 201.

27 Hugh Barker and Yuval Taylor, *Faking It: The Quest for Authenticity in Popular Music* (Norton, 2007), 236.

28 Echols, *Hot Stuff*, 204.

29 Barker and Taylor, *Faking It*, 240.

30 Tim Lawrence, *Life and Death on the New York Dance Floor, 1980–1983* (Duke University Press, 2016), 25.

31 Simon Reynolds, *Rip It Up and Start Again: Postpunk 1978–1984* (Penguin, 2005), 153.

32 Bernard Gendron, *Between Montmartre and the Mudd Club: Popular Music and the Avant-Garde* (University of Chicago Press, 2002), 228.

33 Ibid., 233–34.

34 Ibid., 234.

35 Ibid., 237.

36 Ibid.

37 Ibid., 242.

38 Ibid.

39 Ibid., 258.

40 Theo Cateforis, *Are We Not New Wave? Modern Pop at the Turn of the 1980s* (University of Michigan Press, 2011), 201.

41 Gendron, *Between Montmartre*, 265.

42 Ibid., 265.

43 Barker and Taylor, *Faking It*, 265.

44 Allan F. Moore and Remy Martin, *Rock: The Primary Text* (Routledge, 2018), 159.

45 Ibid., 162.

46 Dave Laing, *One Chord Wonders: Power and Meaning in Punk Rock* (Open University Press, 1985), 63.

47 David Stubbs, *Future Days: Krautrock and the Building of Modern Germany* (Faber & Faber, 2014), 37.

48 Julian Cope, *Krautrocksampler*, 2nd ed. (Head Heritage, 1996), 1.

49 Reynolds, *Rip It*, 2.

50 Mimi Haddon, *What Is Post-Punk? Genre and Identity in Avant-Garde Popular Music, 1977–82* (University of Michigan Press, 2020), 25, 34.

51 Cateforis, *Are We Not*, 1.

52 Ibid., 2.

53 Ibid., 56.

54 Ibid., 62.

55 Ibid., 5.

56 Reynolds, *Rip It*, 24.

57 Ibid.

58 Ibid.

59 Jim Dooley, *Red Set: A History of Gang of Four* (Repeater, 2017), 32.

60 Ibid., 50.

61 Ibid., 83–4.

62 Ibid., 67.

63 Ibid., 86.

64 Ibid., 83.

65 Ibid., 84.

66 Jon Savage, Review of *Entertainment!*, by Gang of Four, *Melody Maker,* October 6, 1979. *Rock's Backpages.*

67 Dooley, *Red Set*, 96.

68 Garry Bushell, "Gang of Four: The Gang's All Here," *Sounds*, June 2, 1979, *Rock's Backpages*; Paul Rambali, Review of *Entertainment!*, by Gang of Four, *New Musical Express,* October 6, 1979. *Rock's Backpages.*

69 Mary Harron, "Gang of Four: Dialectics Meet Disco," *Melody Maker*, May 26, 1979, *Rock's Backpages.*

70 Greil Marcus, *Ranters & Crowd Pleasers: Punk in Pop Music, 1977–92* (Doubleday, 1993), 51.

71 Michael Hoover and Lisa Stokes, "Pop Music and the Limits of Cultural Critique: Gang of Four Shrinkwraps Entertainment," *Popular Music and Society* 22, no. 3 (1998), 21–38.

72 Fred Mills, "Delta 5: Delta Force," *Harp*, March 2006, *Rock's Backpages.*

73 Phil Sutcliffe, "The Delta of Venus: Delta 5," *Sounds*, August 2, 1980, *Rock's Backpages.*

74 Mills, "Delta Force."

75 Reynolds, *Rip It*, 66.

76 Sutcliffe, "The Delta."

77 Ibid.

78 Ibid.

79 Ibid.

80 Mills, "Delta Force."

81 Lucy O'Brien, "Can I Have a Taste of Your Ice Cream?" *Punk & Post Punk* 1, no. 1 (2011), 38.

82 Marcus, *Ranters*, 189–90.

83 Ibid., 191.

84 Vince Aletti, "England's New Slant on Soul," *The Village Voice*, August 5, 1981, 55.

85 David Wilkinson, *Post-Punk, Politics and Pleasure in Britain* (Palgrave Macmillan, 2016), 2.

86 Jim Sullivan, "Liquid Liquid, V: Streets, Boston MA," *The Boston Globe*, December 4, 1981, *Rock's Backpages*.

87 David Stubbs, "The Thin Boys: Post-Punk Funk," *Record Collector*, January 2, 2019, https://recordcollectormag.com/articles/post-punk-funk.

88 Ibid.

89 Reynolds, *Rip It*, 275.

90 Ibid., 227.

91 Ibid., 262.

92 Ibid., 261.

93 Echols, *Hot Stuff*, 216.

94 Ibid., 227.

95 Lawrence, *Life and Death*, ix.

96 Ibid., xiii.

97 Gendron, *Between Montmartre*, 299.

98 Lawrence, *Life and Death*, 38.

99 Ibid., 55.

100 Ibid.

101 Gendron, *Between Montmartre*, 299.

102 Reynolds, *Rip It*, 160.

103 Simon Reynolds, *Totally Wired: Postpunk Interviews and Overviews* (Soft Skull, 2009), 121.

104 Reynolds, *Rip It*, 160.

105 Cateforis, *Are We Not*, 206.

106 Ibid., 207.

107 Gendron, *Between Montmartre*, 286.

108 Peter Silverton, "ZE Records," *New Sounds New Style*, July 1981, *Rock's Backpages*.

109 Paul Rambali, "Why is This Man Hip but a Complete Failure?: Michael Zilkha and ZE Records," *New Musical Express*, December 5, 1981, *Rock's Backpages*.

110 Silverton, "ZE Records."

111 Paul Lester, "ZE Records: 'It Was Like a Fairytale,'" *The Guardian*, July 30, 2009, https://www.theguardian.com/music/2009/jul/30/ze-records.

112 Reynolds, *Rip It*, 268.

113 Rambali, "Why."

114 Shapiro, *Turn the Beat Around*, xvii.

115 Lawrence, *Life and Death*, 15.

116 Reynolds, *Rip It*, 150.

117 Lawrence, *Life and Death*, 15.

118 Reynolds, *Rip It*, 150.

119 Reynolds, *Totally Wired*, 135.

120 Reynolds, *Rip It*, 154.

121 Ibid., 156–57.

122 Lawrence, *Life and Death*, 94.

123 Ibid., 95.

124 Tim Ross, "Something Like a Phenomenon: The Complete 99 Records Story," *Tuba Frenzy*, no. 4 (Spring 1998), 22.

125 Mike Rubin, "The 99 Records Story," *Red Bull Music Academy*, May 19, 2013, https://daily.redbullmusicacademy. com/2013/05/99-records-feature.

126 Reynolds, *Rip It*, 272.

127 Ross, "Something," 27–8.

128 Richard Grabel, "The Bush Tetras: Outsiders in a Sexual Jungle," *New Musical Express*, November 8, 1980, *Rock's Backpages*.

129 Ross, "Something," 23.

130 Vivien Goldman, *Revenge of the She-Punks: A Feminist Music History from Poly Styrene to Pussy Riot* (University of Texas Press, 2019), 48.

131 Ibid.

132 Ibid.

133 Reynolds, *Rip It*, 274.

134 Lawrence, *Life and Death*, 211.

135 Anna Wilson, "The Legendary Liquid Liquid—Interview, Part 1," *Clash*, August 6, 2010, https://www.clashmusic. com/features/the-legendary-liquid-liquid-interview-part-1.

136 Anna Wilson, "The Legendary Liquid Liquid—Interview, Part 2," *Clash*, August 6, 2010, https://www.clashmusic.com/ features/the-legendary-liquid-liquid-interview-part-2.

137 Reynolds, *Rip It*, 273.

138 Kembrew McLeod and Peter DiCola, *Creative License: The Law and Culture of Digital Sampling* (Duke University Press, 2011), 112.

139 "Sal Principato on Liquid Liquid's Optimo," *Ban Ban Ton Ton*, April 30, 2020, https://banbantonton.com/2020/04/30/sal-principato-on-liquid-liquids-optimo/.

140 Sullivan, "Liquid Liquid."

141 "Sal Principato."

142 Reynolds, *Rip It*, 274.

143 Ibid.

144 Goldman, *Revenge*, 63–4.

145 Reynolds, *Rip It*, 272.

146 Lawrence, *Life and Death*, 212.

147 Goldman, *Revenge*, 64–5.

148 Richard Grabel, "ESG: No Guile or Wile, Just Wallop," *New Musical Express*, May 23, 1981, *Rock's Backpages*.

149 Lawrence, *Life and Death*, 213.

150 Ibid., 315.

151 Ibid., 343.

152 Ibid., 400–1.

153 McLeod and DiCola, *Creative License*, 113.

154 Lawrence, *Life and Death*, xii.

155 Reynolds, *Rip It*, 390.

156 Reynolds, *Totally Wired*, 412–13.

Chapter 3

1 Hugh Barker and Yuval Taylor, *Faking It: The Quest for Authenticity in Popular Music* (Norton, 2007), 254.

2 Simon Reynolds, *Rip It Up and Start Again: Postpunk 1978–1984* (Penguin, 2005), 69.

3 Kevin Mattson, *We're Not Here to Entertain: Punk Rock, Ronald Reagan, and the Real Culture War of 1980s America* (Oxford University Press, 2020).

4 David Hesmondhalgh, "Indie: The Institutional Politics and Aesthetics of a Popular Music Genre," *Cultural Studies* 13, no. 1 (1999), 34–61.

5 David Wilkinson, *Post-Punk, Politics and Pleasure in Britain* (Palgrave Macmillan, 2016), 190–91.

6 David Balzer, *Curationism: How Curating Took Over the Art World and Everything Else* (Coach House, 2014), 46.

7 Ibid., 8.

8 Ibid., 8–9.

9 Ibid., 9.

10 Ibid., 121.

11 Ibid., 76.

12 Dayna Tortorici, "You Know It When You See It," in *What Was the Hipster? A Sociological Investigation*, ed. Mark Greif, Kathleen Ross, and Dayna Tortorici (n+1 Foundation, 2010), 122–23.

13 Mark Greif, "Positions," in *What Was the Hipster? A Sociological Investigation*, ed. Mark Greif, Kathleen Ross, and Dayna Tortorici (n+1 Foundation, 2010), 9–12.

14 Ibid., 9–10.

15 Ibid., 10–11.

16 Ibid., 12.

17 Ibid., 9.

18 Jake Kinzey, *The Sacred and the Profane: An Investigation of Hipsters* (Zer0 Books, 2012), 2.

19 Heike Steinhoff, "Hipster Culture: A Definition," in *Hipster Culture: Transnational and Intersectional Perspectives*, ed. Heike Steinhoff (Bloomsbury, 2021), 8.

20 Greif, "Positions," 6.

21 Richard A. Peterson, "Understanding Audience Segmentation: From Elite and Mass to Omnivore and Univore," *Poetics* 21, no. 4 (1992), 243–58.

22 Balzer, *Curationism*, 122.

23 Ibid.

24 Lizzy Goodman, *Meet Me in the Bathroom: Rebirth and Rock and Roll in New York City 2001–2011* (Dey St., 2017), 456.

25 Kinzey, *Sacred*, 3.

26 Wilkinson, *Post-Punk*, 191.

27 Reynolds, *Rip It*, 398.

28 Todd Naylor, "Disco Punk Explosion!" *Muzik*, April 2003, 34–6.

29 Simon Reynolds, Review of *They Threw Us All in a Trench and Stuck a Monument on Top*, by Liars, *Uncut,* September 2002, *Rock's Backpages*.

30 Andy Greenwald, "Where's Brooklyn at?" *Spin*, July 2002, 85.

31 Ibid., 86.

32 Ibid.

33 Jody Rosen, "The End of LCD Soundsystem: How a chubby 'old' guy became king of the hipsters," *Slate*, April 4, 2011, https://slate.com/culture/2011/04/lcd-soundsystem-how-a-chubby-old-guy-became-king-of-the-hipsters.html.

34 Matt McDermott, "Rewind: The Rapture—House of Jealous Lovers," *Resident Advisor*, September 14, 2019, https://ra.co/reviews/24209.

35 Goodman, *Meet Me*, 88–9.

36 Ibid., 87.

37 Ibid., 51.

38 Ibid., 57.

39 Ibid., 401.

40 David Madden, "Cross-Dressing to Backbeats: The Status of the Electroclash Producer and the Politics of Electronic Music," *Dancecult* 4, no. 2 (2012), 28.

41 Goodman, *Meet Me*, 75.

42 Madden, "Cross-Dressing," 28.

43 Lucy O'Brien, "Can I Have a Taste of Your Ice Cream?" *Punk & Post Punk* 1, no. 1 (2011), 39.

44 Caryn Ganz, "Rebels Without a Pause," *Spin*, October 2004, 87.

45 Ibid.

46 Nick Sylvester, "Review of *DFA Records Presents: Compilation #1*, by DFA Records," *Pitchfork*, December 9, 2003, https://pitchfork.com/reviews/albums/2031-dfa-records-presents-compilation-1/.

47 Goodman, *Meet Me*, 85.

48 Ibid., 265.

49 Tony Ware, "The Rapture's Luke Jenner on Living in San Francisco, Being the 'Black Sheep' of Sub Pop, and Learning to Be Positive," *SF Weekly*, October 7, 2011, https://archives.sfweekly.com/shookdown/2011/10/07/the-raptures-luke-jenner-on-living-in-san-francisco-being-the-black-sheep-of-sub-pop-and-learning-to-be-positive.

50 David Strauss, "Groove is in the Art: An interview with !!!'s Nic Offer," *Electronic Beats*, April 25, 2013, https://www.electronicbeats.net/an-interview-with-nic-offer/.

51 Sianne Ngai, *Ugly Feelings* (Harvard University Press, 2007).

52 William Van Meter, "LCD Soundsystem," *Spin*, February 2005, 55.

53 Ruvan Wijesooriya, *LCD* (Powerhouse, 2021).

54 Ryan Leas, *LCD Soundsystem's Sound of Silver* (Bloomsbury, 2016), 13.

55 Ibid.

56 Hamilton Harvey, *Franz Ferdinand and the Pop Renaissance* (Reynolds & Hearn, 2005), 159.

57 Goodman, *Meet Me*, 356.

58 Andy Greenwald, "The Big Tease," *Spin*, October 2004, 74.

59 Goodman, *Meet Me*, 357.

60 Marc Spitz, "Franz Ferdinand," *Spin*, November 2005, 60.

61 Greenwald, "Tease," 73.

62 Alex Needham, "Morrissey: 'Are you enjoying the hysteria?' Alex: 'Yeah, we're loving it.'" *New Musical Express*, May 22, 2004, 27.

63 Wilkinson, *Post-Punk*, 191.

64 Douglas McWilliams, *The Flat White Economy: How the Digital Economy Is Transforming London and Other Cities of the Future* (Duckworth Overlook, 2015).

65 Nick Southall, Review of *Silent Alarm*, by Bloc Party, *The Stylus*, February 14, 2005.

66 Jude Rogers, Review of *Silent Alarm*, by Bloc Party. *The Word*, March 2005, *Rock's Backpages*.

67 Chris Hawke, "Next Big Thing Tames Marxist Innovations to Rock the Party," *The Village Voice* 50, no. 14 (2005), C92.

68 Sarah Lewitinn and Charles Aaron, "15 More to Watch: British Rock," *Spin*, February 2005, 73.

69 Alex Petridis, "'This Is Going to Look Really Bad,'" *The Guardian*, October 7, 2005, https://www.theguardian.com/music/2005/oct/07/popandrock.blocparty.

70 Emily Shelton, "Q and Not U's Recreation Myth," *WVAU*, October 26, 2017, http://wvau.org/3661/archives/q-and-not-us-recreation-myth/.

71 Jessica Grose, "Test Icicles," *Spin*, November 2, 2005, https://www.spin.com/2005/11/test-icicles/.

72 Lina Abascal, *Never Be Alone Again: How Bloghouse United the Internet and the Dancefloor* (Two Palms, 2021), 20.

73 Todd Naylor, "This Is New Rave," *New Musical Express*, June 17, 2006, 22–4.

74 "House of Rapture Lovers," *New Musical Express*, September 2, 2006, 19.

75 Naylor, "This," 22–4.

76 Scott Wilson, Chal Ravens, April Clare Welsh, and Tam Gunn, "What the Hell Was Blog House? 30 Classic Tracks from a Great Lost Era," *FACT Magazine*, June 16, 2016, https://www.factmag.com/2016/06/16/30-best-blog-house-tracks/.

77 Abascal, *Never*, 2.

78 Larissa Wodtke, "MP3 as Contentious Message: When Infinite Repetition Fuses with the Acoustic Sphere," in *Seriality and Texts for Young People: The Compulsion to Repeat*, ed. Mavis Reimer, Nyala Ali, Deanna England, and Melanie Dennis Unrau (Palgrave, 2014), 237–57.

Chapter 4

1 Mimi Haddon, *What Is Post-Punk? Genre and Identity in Avant-Garde Popular Music, 1977–82* (University of Michigan Press, 2020), 4.

2   Michael Veal, *Dub: Soundscapes and Shattered Songs in Jamaican Reggae* (Wesleyean University Press, 2013).

3   Simon Reynolds, *Rip It Up and Start Again: Postpunk 1978–1984* (Penguin, 2005), 4.

4   Jim Dooley, *Red Set: A History of Gang of Four* (Repeater, 2017), 343.

5   Ibid., 343–4.

6   John Pawson and Lucy Orta, "To be minimalist … or maximalist?" *The Guardian*, April 19, 2004, https://www.theguardian.com/culture/2004/apr/19/guesteditors1.

7   Simon Reynolds, *Totally Wired: Postpunk Interviews and Overviews* (Soft Skull, 2009), 121.

8   Dooley, *Red Set*, 93.

9   Tim Lawrence, *Life and Death on the New York Dance Floor, 1980–1983* (Duke University Press, 2016), 212.

10   Robert Loss, *Nothing Has Been Done Before: Seeking the New in 21st-Century American Popular Music* (Bloomsbury, 2017), https://doi.org/10.5040/9781501322051.ch-008.

11   Reynolds, *Rip It*, 214.

12   Dooley, *Red Set*, 80.

13   Ibid., 95.

14   John Leland, *Hip: The History* (Harper, 2004), 102.

15   Lawrence, *Life and Death*, 211.

16   "Sal Principato on Liquid Liquid's Optimo," *Ban Ban Ton Ton*, April 30, 2020, https://banbantonton.com/2020/04/30/sal-principato-on-liquid-liquids-optimo/.

17   Mike Rubin, "The 99 Records Story," *Red Bull Music Academy*, May 19, 2013, https://daily.redbullmusicacademy.com/2013/05/99-records-feature.

18 Kevin Dettmar, *Gang of Four's Entertainment!* (Bloomsbury, 2014), http://dx.doi.org/10.5040/9781501396908.

19 Ibid.

20 Reynolds, *Rip It*, 3.

21 Ibid.

22 Daryl Easlea, *Everybody Dance: Chic and the Politics of Disco* (Omnibus, 2020), 46.

23 Dooley, *Red Set*, 80–1.

24 Lucy O'Brien, "Can I Have a Taste of Your Ice Cream?," *Punk & Post Punk* 1, no. 1 (2011), 29.

25 Brenda Dixon Gottschild, *The Black Dancing Body: A Geography from Coon to Cool* (Palgrave, 2003), 16.

26 Adriana Cavarero, *Inclinations: A Critique of Rectitude*, trans. Amanda Minervini and Adam Sitze (Stanford University Press, 2016).

27 Leland, *Hip*, 119.

28 Dooley, *Red Set*, 86.

29 Reynolds, *Rip It*, 57.

30 Reynolds, *Totally Wired*, 116.

31 Ibid., 125.

32 Mark Fisher (K-Punk), "Rhythm Infections: Liquid Liquid's Ecstatic, Eerie Funk," *Fact Magazine*, March 10, 2008, https://web.archive.org/web/20080310052748/http://www.factmagazine.co.uk/da/73047.

33 Mark Abel, *Groove: An Aesthetic of Measured Time* (Brill, 2014), 1.

34 Ibid.

35 Ibid., 17.

36 Ibid., 23.

37 Ibid., 244.

38 Tiger C. Roholt, *Groove: A Phenomenology of Rhythmic Nuance* (Bloomsbury, 2014), 2.

39 "Syncopation in pop/rock music." *Open Music Theory*, http://openmusictheory.com/syncopation.html.

40 Jeremy Gilbert and Ewan Pearson, *Discographies: Dance, Music, Culture and the Politics of Sound* (Routledge, 1999), 6.

41 Catherine Clément, *Syncope: The Philosophy of Rapture*, trans. Sally O'Driscoll and Deirdre M. Mahoney (University of Minnesota Press, 1994), 2.

42 Ibid., 5.

43 Ibid., 7.

44 Ibid., 31.

45 Andy Greenwald, "The Big Tease," *Spin* (October 2004), 77.

46 Clément, *Syncope*, 49.

47 Theo Cateforis, *Are We Not New Wave? Modern Pop at the Turn of the 1980s* (University of Michigan Press, 2011), 33.

48 Reynolds, *Rip It*, 63–4.

49 Ibid., 119.

50 Ibid., 167.

51 Lizzy Goodman, *Meet Me in the Bathroom: Rebirth and Rock and Roll in New York City 2001–2011* (Dey St., 2017), 264.

52 Gemma Pike, "Bloc Party frontman Kele Okereke on Silent Alarm's biggest tracks," *The J Files*, May 14, 2020, https://www.abc.net.au/doublej/music-reads/features/bloc-party-silent-alarm-kele-okereke/12248212.

53 Ibid.

54 O'Brien, "Can I," 31.

55 Reynolds, *Rip It*, 68.

56 Northrop Frye, "Literature as a Critique of Pure Reason," in *The Secular Scripture and Other Writings on Critical Theory*, ed. Joseph Adamson and Jean Wilson (University of Toronto Press, 2006), 232.

57 Ibid.

58 T. E. Hulme, "Romanticism and Classicism," *Poetry Foundation*, https://www.poetryfoundation.org/articles/69477/romanticism-and-classicism.

59 Sianne Ngai, *Our Aesthetic Categories: Zany, Cute, Interesting* (Harvard University Press, 2012), 172.

60 Rob Young, "Liquid Ecstasy: LCD Soundsystem: LCD Soundsystem," *Uncut*, February 2005, *Rock's Backpages*.

61 Noreen Masud, "A Horizon Line: Flat Style in Contemporary Women's Poetry," *Textual Practice* (2022), 3.

62 Simon Frith and Howard Horne, *Art into Pop* (Methuen, 1987), 7.

63 Masud, "Horizon Line," 4.

64 Lauren Berlant, "Structures of Unfeeling: *Mysterious Skin*," *International Journal of Politics, Culture, and Society* 28 (2015), 198; Sianne Ngai, "Stuplimity: Shock and Boredom in Twentieth-Century Aesthetics," *Postmodern Culture* 10, no. 2 (2000).

65 Ngai, "Stuplimity."

66 Rob Horning, "The Primitive Accumulation of Cool," *The New Inquiry*, June 4, 2013, https://thenewinquiry.com/blog/the-primitive-accumulation-of-cool/.

67 Allan F. Moore and Remy Martin, *Rock: The Primary Text* (Routledge, 2018), 44.

68 Fisher, "Rhythm."

69 Daniel Herwitz, "The New Spaces of Modernist Painting," in *The Cambridge History of Modernism*, ed. Vincent Sherry

(Cambridge University Press, 2017).; Kai Mikkonen, "Artificial Africa in the European Avant-Garde: Marinetti and Tzara," in *Europa! Europa? The Avant Garde, Modernism and the Fate of the Continent*, ed. Sascha Bru, Jan Baetens, Benedikt Hjartarson, Peter Nicholls, Tania Ørum, and Hubert van den Berg (De Gruyter, 2009), 391–407.

70 Fisher, "Rhythm."

71 Brendan M. Gillen, "Sal Principato (Liquid Liquid)," *Red Bull Music Academy*, 2003, https://www.redbullmusicacademy. com/lectures/sal-principato-something-like-a-phenomenon.

72 Walter Hughes, "In the Empire of the Beat: Discipline and Disco," in *Electronica, Club and Dance Music*, ed. Mark J. Butler (Routledge, 2012), 135.

73 Gilbert and Pearson, *Discographies*, 15.

74 Dooley, *Red Set*, 105.

75 Ibid., 396.

76 Lawrence, *Life and Death*, 475–9.

77 Reynolds, *Totally Wired*, 413.

78 James Murphy, "On Losing One's Edge," *Five Dials*, no. 13 (2009), 9.

79 Kele Okereke, "The Kick," *Five Dials*, no. 13 (2009), 21–3.

80 Kele Okereke, "Shoplifting," in *Punk Fiction: An Anthology of Short Stories Inspired by Punk*, ed. Janine Bullman (Portico, 2009), 32–8.; Dev Hynes, "The KKK Took My Baby Away," in *Punk Fiction: An Anthology of Short Stories Inspired by Punk*, ed. Janine Bullman (Portico, 2009), 224–30.

81 Alex Kapranos, *Sound Bites: Eating on Tour with Franz Ferdinand* (Penguin, 2006).

82 Reynolds, *Totally Wired*, 411.

83 Dettmar, *Gang*, http://dx.doi.org/10.5040/9781501396908.

84 Reynolds, *Rip It*, 68.

85 Richard Grabel, "The Bush Tetras: Outsiders in a Sexual Jungle," *New Musical Express*, November 8, 1980, *Rock's Backpages*.

86 Sianne Ngai, *Ugly Feelings* (Harvard University Press, 2007), 299.

87 Ibid., 302.

88 Dettmar, *Gang*, http://dx.doi.org/10.5040/9781501396908.

89 Ryan Leas, *LCD Soundsystem's Sound of Silver* (Bloomsbury, 2016), 24.

90 Paul Morley, "Au Pairs: Every Home Should Have Four," *New Musical Express*, October 11, 1980. *Rock's Backpages*.

91 Larissa Wodtke, "The Irony and the Ecstasy: The Queer Aging of Pet Shop Boys and LCD Soundsystem in Electronic Dance Music," *Dancecult* 11, no. 1 (2019), 31.

92 Andrew Calcutt, *Arrested Development: Pop Culture and the Erosion of Adulthood* (Bloomsbury, 1998), 175.

93 Leas, *LCD*, 41.

94 Dettmar, *Gang*, http://dx.doi.org/10.5040/9781501396908.

95 David Wilkinson, *Post-Punk, Politics and Pleasure in Britain* (Palgrave Macmillan, 2016), 192.

Chapter 5

1 Lester Bangs, "The White Noise Supremacists," *The Village Voice*, April 30, 1979, 45–7.

2 Sasha Frere-Jones, "A Paler Shade of White," *New Yorker Magazine*, October 22, 2007, https://www.newyorker.com/magazine/2007/10/22/a-paler-shade-of-white.

3 Mark Abel, *Groove: An Aesthetic of Measured Time* (Brill, 2014), 77.

4 Mimi Haddon, *What Is Post-Punk? Genre and Identity in Avant-Garde Popular Music, 1977–82* (University of Michigan Press, 2020), 41.

5 Ibid., 60.

6 Ibid., 63.

7 Christopher Partridge, *Dub in Babylon: Understanding the Evolution and Significance of Dub Reggae in Jamaica and Britain from King Tubby to Post-Punk* (Equinox, 2010), 247.

8 "Leaders of the New School," *Muzik*, April 2003, 37.

9 John Leland, *Hip: The History* (Harper, 2004), 65.

10 Alan Platt, "No Chance," *SoHo Weekly News*, January 7, 1979, 39.

11 Reynolds, *Totally Wired*, 138.

12 Ibid.

13 Ibid., 133.

14 Michael Crumsho, "Dance Class: An Interview with Out Hud," *Dusted Magazine*, http://www.dustedmagazine.com/features/68.

15 Simon Reynolds, *Rip It Up and Start Again: Postpunk 1978–1984* (Penguin, 2005), 155.

16 Robin James, "In but not of, of but not in: On Taste, Hipness, and White Embodiment," *Contemporary Aesthetics* 2, 2009, https://contempaesthetics.org/newvolume/pages/article.php?articleID=549.

17 Phil Ford, *Dig: Sound and Music in Hip Culture* (Oxford University Press, 2013), 54.

18 James, "In but not of."

19 Ibid.

20 Tim Lawrence, *Life and Death on the New York Dance Floor, 1980–1983* (Duke University Press, 2016), 25.

21 Ibid., 158.

22 Lizzy Goodman, *Meet Me in the Bathroom: Rebirth and Rock and Roll in New York City 2001–2011* (Dey St., 2017), 51.

23 Reynolds, *Rip It*, 213.

24 Haddon, *What*, 78.

25 Ryan Leas, *LCD Soundsystem's Sound of Silver* (Bloomsbury, 2016), 18.

26 Haddon, *What*, 88.

27 Alice Echols, *Hot Stuff: Disco and the Remaking of American Culture* (W. W. Norton, 2010), 220.

28 Brenda Dixon Gottschild, *The Black Dancing Body: A Geography from Coon to Cool* (Palgrave, 2003), 21.

29 Reynolds, *Rip It*, 3.

30 Tim Sommer, "Liquid Liquid: The Most Important NY Band You've Never Heard Of," *The Observer*, July 16, 2015, https://observer.com/2015/07/liquid-liquid-the-most-important-ny-band-youve-never-heard-of/.

31 Reynolds, *Rip It*, 160.

32 Richard Grabel, "ESG: No Guile or Wile, Just Wallop," *New Musical Express*, May 23, 1981, *Rock's Backpages*.

33 Mark Fisher (K-Punk), "Rhythm Infections: Liquid Liquid's Ecstatic, Eerie Funk," *Fact Magazine*, March 10, 2008, https://web.archive.org/web/20080310052748/http://www.factmagazine.co.uk/da/73047.

34 Haddon, *What*, 91.

35 Ibid., 93.

36 Ibid., 95–6.

37 Theo Cateforis, *Are We Not New Wave? Modern Pop at the Turn of the 1980s* (University of Michigan Press, 2011), 75.

38 Ibid., 80.

39 Brenda Dixon Gottschild, *Digging the Africanist Presence in American Performance: Dance and Other Contexts* (Greenwood Press, 1996), 9.

40 Mitchell Cohen, Review of *Remain in Light*, by Talking Heads, *Creem*, January 1981, *Rock's Backpages*.

41 Paul Morley, "Au Pairs: Every Home Should Have Four," *New Musical Express*, October 11, 1980. *Rock's Backpages*.

42 Richard Grabel, "The Bush Tetras: Outsiders in a Sexual Jungle," *New Musical Express*, November 8, 1980, *Rock's Backpages*.

43 Leas, *LCD*, 29.

44 Pat Long, Review of *Pieces of the People We Love*, by The Rapture. *New Musical Express*, September 2, 2006, 19.

45 Phil Sutcliffe, "The Delta of Venus: Delta 5," *Sounds*, August 2, 1980, *Rock's Backpages*.

46 Barney Hoskyns, Review of *Yes New York/New York Noise/Post Punk 01*, by Various Artists. *Uncut,* 2003, *Rock's Backpages*.

47 Lawrence, *Life and Death*, 408.

48 Ibid.

49 Kembrew McLeod and Peter DiCola, *Creative License: The Law and Culture of Digital Sampling* (Duke University Press, 2011), 114.

50 Vivien Goldman, *Revenge of the She-Punks: A Feminist Music History from Poly Styrene to Pussy Riot* (University of Texas Press, 2019), 65.

51 Brendan M. Gillen, "Sal Principato (Liquid Liquid)," *Red Bull Music Academy*, 2003, https://www.redbullmusicacademy. com/lectures/sal-principato-something-like-a-phenomenon.

52 Tara Brabazon, *From Revolution to Revelation: Generation X, Popular Memory and Cultural Studies* (Ashgate, 2005), 106.

53 Ibid.

54 Lucy O'Brien, "Can I Have a Taste of Your Ice Cream?," *Punk & Post Punk* 1, no. 1 (2011), 28.

55 Reynolds, *Rip It*, 65.

56 O'Brien, "Can I," 33.

57 Haddon, *What*, 106.

58 Grabel, "Bush Tetras."

59 Dan Fox, *Pretentiousness: Why It Matters* (Coffee House, 2016), 70.

60 Goodman, *Meet*, 75.

61 Ibid., 78.

62 Simon Reynolds, *Retromania: Pop Culture's Addiction to Its Own Past* (Faber and Faber, 2011), 173.

63 Stephen Daw, "2002: How Electroclash Redefined the Queer Music Scene," *Billboard*, March 24, 2022.

64 Ryan Schreiber, Review of *Echoes*, by The Rapture. *Pitchfork*, September 9, 2003, https://pitchfork.com/reviews/albums/6693-echoes/.

65 Dick Pountain and David Robins, *Cool Rules: Anatomy of an Attitude* (Reaktion, 2000), 19.

66 Ibid., 26.

67 Ibid., 21.

68 Vanessa Brown, "Is Coolness Still Cool?," *Journal for Cultural Research* 25, no. 4 (2021), 430.

69 Ibid.

70 Ibid., 432.

71 Ibid., 434.

72 Grégory Pierrot, *Decolonize Hipsters* (OR Books, 2021), 31.

73 Ibid., 45.

74 Ibid., 93.

75 Ibid., 47.

76 Shannon Winnubst, *Way Too Cool: Selling Out Race and Ethics* (Columbia University Press, 2015), 20.

77 Ibid., 13.

78 Ibid., 37.

79 Ibid., 38.

80 Ibid., 87.

81 Ibid., 102.

Afterword

1 Anton Spice, "Funk in Opposition: The Post-punk Dance Continuum from 1977 to the Present Day," *WaxPoetics*, October 6, 2021, https://www.waxpoetics.com/article/the-post-punk-dance-continuum-from-1977-to-the-present-day/.

2 Allison P. Davis, "A Vibe Shift Is Coming: Will Any of Us Survive It?" *The Cut*, February 16, 2022, https://www.thecut.com/2022/02/a-vibe-shift-is-coming.html; Daniel Rodgers, "WTF Is Indie Sleaze and Is It Actually Making a Comeback?" *Dazed*, October 29, 2021, https://www.dazeddigital.com/fashion/article/54603/1/wtf-is-indie-sleaze-comeback-tiktok-trend-y2k-chanel-saint-laurent-cobrasnake.

3 Carl Wilson, "A Guide to Music Jargon," *The Globe and Mail*, January 8, 2005, R4.

4   Simon Reynolds, *Retromania: Pop Culture's Addiction to Its Own Past* (Faber and Faber, 2011), 173.

5   Lizzy Goodman, *Meet Me in the Bathroom: Rebirth and Rock and Roll in New York City 2001–2011* (Dey St., 2017), 288.

6   Robert Loss, *Nothing Has Been Done Before: Seeking the New in 21st-Century American Popular Music* (Bloomsbury, 2017), https://doi.org/10.5040/9781501322051.ch-008.

7   Dayo Olopade, "The Hipster," in *Black Cool: One Thousand Streams of Blackness*, ed. Rebecca Walker (Soft Skull Press, 2012), 44.

8   David Harvie and Keir Milburn, "The Zombie of Neoliberalism can be Beaten—through mass direct Action," *The Guardian*, August 4, 2011, https://www.theguardian.com/commentisfree/2011/aug/04/neoliberalism-zombie-action-phone-hacking.

9   Douglas Rushkoff, *Present Shock: When Everything Happens Now* (Current, 2013), 4.

10   Ibid., 197–241.

11   William David James Rees, "Future Nostalgia? 21st Century Disco," *Dancecult* 13, no. 1 (2021), 36–53, https://dj.dancecult.net/index.php/dancecult/article/view/1195/1015.

12   Madeline Roth, "Bloc Party's Kele Okereke on Their 'Cold' New Album: 'Everyone's F-cking Everyone Over'," *The Daily Beast*, May 1, 2022, https://www.thedailybeast.com/bloc-partys-kele-okereke-on-the-ugly-fury-behind-alpha-games.

13   Miles Raymer, "Control, Chaos, and the Fury of Bloc Party's 'Silent Alarm'," *Riot Fest*, July 2, 2019, https://riotfest.org/2019/07/02/control-chaos-bloc-party/.

Bibliography

Abascal, Lina. *Never Be Alone Again: How Bloghouse United the Internet and the Dancefloor*. New York: Two Palms, 2021.

Abel, Mark. *Groove: An Aesthetic of Measured Time*. Leiden: Brill, 2014.

Aletti, Vince. "England's New Slant on Soul." *The Village Voice*, August 5, 1981.

Balzer, David. *Curationism: How Curating Took Over the Art World and Everything Else*. Toronto: Coach House, 2014.

Bangs, Lester. "The White Noise Supremacists." *The Village Voice*, April 30, 1979.

Barker, Hugh, and Yuval Taylor. *Faking It: The Quest for Authenticity in Popular Music*. New York: Norton, 2007.

Berlant, Lauren. "Structures of Unfeeling: *Mysterious Skin*." *International Journal of Politics, Culture, and Society* 28 (2015): 191–213.

Brabazon, Tara. *From Revolution to Revelation: Generation X, Popular Memory and Cultural Studies*. Aldershot: Ashgate, 2005.

Brown, Vanessa. "Is Coolness Still Cool?" *Journal for Cultural Research* 25, no. 4 (2021): 429–45.

Bushell, Garry. "Gang of Four: The Gang's All Here." *Sounds*, June 2, 1979, *Rock's Backpages*.

Calcutt, Andrew. *Arrested Development: Pop Culture and the Erosion of Adulthood*. London: Bloomsbury, 1998.

Cateforis, Theo. *Are We Not New Wave? Modern Pop at the Turn of the 1980s*. Ann Arbor: University of Michigan Press, 2011.

Cavarero, Adriana. *Inclinations: A Critique of Rectitude*. Translated by Amanda Minervini and Adam Sitze. Stanford: Stanford University Press, 2016.

Clément, Catherine. *Syncope: The Philosophy of Rapture*. Translated by Sally O'Driscoll and Deirdre M. Mahoney. Minneapolis: University of Minnesota Press, 1994.

Cohen, Mitchell. "Review of *Remain in Light*, by Talking Heads." *Creem*, January 1981, *Rock's Backpages*.

Cope, Julian. *Krautrocksampler*. 2nd ed. Yatesbury: Head Heritage, 1996.

Crumsho, Michael. "Dance Class: An Interview with Out Hud." *Dusted Magazine*, http://www.dustedmagazine.com/features/68.

Davis, Allison P. "A Vibe Shift Is Coming: Will Any of Us Survive It?" *The Cut*, February 16, 2022, https://www.thecut.com/2022/02/a-vibe-shift-is-coming.html.

Daw, Stephen. "2002: How Electroclash Redefined the Queer Music Scene." *Billboard*, March 24, 2022.

Dettmar, Kevin. *Gang of Four's Entertainment!* New York: Bloomsbury, 2014, http://dx.doi.org/10.5040/9781501396908.

Dinerstein, Joel. *The Origins of Cool in Postwar America*. Chicago: University of Chicago Press, 2017.

Dooley, Jim. *Red Set: A History of Gang of Four*. London: Repeater, 2017.

Dyer, Richard. "In Defence of Disco." *Gay Left*, no. 8 (1979): 20–3.

Easlea, Daryl. *Everybody Dance: Chic and the Politics of Disco*. London: Omnibus, 2020.

Echols, Alice. *Hot Stuff: Disco and the Remaking of American Culture*. New York: W. W. Norton, 2010.

Fisher, Mark (K-Punk). "Rhythm Infections: Liquid Liquid's Ecstatic, Eerie Funk." *Fact Magazine*, March 10, 2008, https://web.archive.org/web/20080310052748/http://www.factmagazine.co.uk/da/73047.

Fonarow, Wendy. *Empire of Dirt: The Aesthetics and Rituals of British Indie Music*. Middletown: Wesleyan University Press, 2006.

Ford, Phil. *Dig: Sound and Music in Hip Culture*. New York: Oxford University Press, 2013.

Fox, Dan. *Pretentiousness: Why It Matters*. Minneapolis: Coffee House, 2016.

Fraiman, Susan. *Cool Men and the Second Sex*. New York: Columbia University Press, 2003.

Frere-Jones, Sasha. "A Paler Shade of White." *New Yorker Magazine*, October 22, 2007, https://www.newyorker.com/magazine/2007/10/22/a-paler-shade-of-white.

Frith, Simon, and Howard Horne. *Art into Pop*. London: Methuen, 1985.

Frye, Northrop. "Literature as a Critique of Pure Reason." In *The Secular Scripture and Other Writings on Critical Theory*, 230–44. Edited by Joseph Adamson and Jean Wilson. Toronto: University of Toronto Press, 2006.

Ganz, Caryn. "Rebels Without a Pause." *Spin*, October 2004.

Gendron, Bernard. *Between Montmartre and the Mudd Club: Popular Music and the Avant-Garde*. Chicago: University of Chicago Press, 2002.

Gilbert, Jeremy, and Ewan Pearson. *Discographies: Dance, Music, Culture and the Politics of Sound*. London: Routledge, 1999.

Gillen, Brendan M. "Sal Principato (Liquid Liquid)." *Red Bull Music Academy*, 2003, https://www.redbullmusicacademy.com/lectures/sal-principato-something-like-a-phenomenon.

Goldman, Vivien. *Revenge of the She-Punks: A Feminist Music History from Poly Styrene to Pussy Riot*. Austin: University of Texas Press, 2019.

Goodman, Lizzie. *Meet Me in the Bathroom: Rebirth and Rock and Roll in New York City 2001–2011*. New York: Dey St., 2017.

Gottschild, Brenda Dixon. *Digging the Africanist Presence in American Performance: Dance and Other Contexts*. Westport: Greenwood Press, 1996.

Gottschild, Brenda Dixon. *The Black Dancing Body: A Geography from Coon to Cool*. New York: Palgrave Macmillan, 2003.

Grabel, Richard. "The Bush Tetras: Outsiders in a Sexual Jungle." *New Musical Express*, November 8, 1980, *Rock's Backpages*.

Grabel, Richard. "ESG: No Guile or Wile, Just Wallop." *New Musical Express*, May 23, 1981, *Rock's Backpages*.

Greenwald, Andy. "Where's Brooklyn at?" *Spin*, July 2002.

Greenwald, Andy. "The Big Tease." *Spin*, October 2004.

Greif, Mark. "Positions." In *What Was the Hipster? A Sociological Investigation*, 4–13. Edited by Mark, Greif, Kathleen Ross, and Dayna Tortorici. New York: n+1 Foundation, 2010.

Grose, Jessica. "Test Icicles." *Spin*, November 2, 2005, https://www.spin.com/2005/11/test-icicles/.

Haddon, Mimi. *What Is Post-Punk? Genre and Identity in Avant-Garde Popular Music, 1977–82*. Ann Arbor: University of Michigan Press, 2020.

Harron, Mary. "Gang of Four: Dialectics Meet Disco." *Melody Maker*, May 26, 1979, *Rock's Backpages*.

Harvey, David. *A Brief History of Neoliberalism*. Oxford: Oxford University Press, 2007.

Harvey, Hamilton. *Franz Ferdinand and the Pop Renaissance*. London: Reynolds & Hearn, 2005.

Harvie, David, and Keir Milburn. "The Zombie of Neoliberalism Can Be Beaten—Through Mass Direct Action." *The*

Guardian, August 4, 2011, https://www.theguardian.com/commentisfree/2011/aug/04/neoliberalism-zombie-action-phone-hacking.

Hawke, Chris. "Next Big Thing Tames Marxist Innovations to Rock the Party." *The Village Voice* 50, no. 14 (2005): C92.

Herwitz, Daniel. "The New Spaces of Modernist Painting." In *The Cambridge History of Modernism*, 181–99. Edited by Vincent Sherry. Cambridge: Cambridge University Press, 2017.

Hesmondhalgh, David. "Indie: The Institutional Politics and Aesthetics of a Popular Music Genre." *Cultural Studies* 13, no. 1 (1999): 34–61.

Hoover, Michael, and Lisa Stokes. "Pop Music and the Limits of Cultural Critique: Gang of Four Shrinkwraps Entertainment." *Popular Music and Society* 22, no. 3 (1998): 21–38.

Horning, Rob. "The Primitive Accumulation of Cool." *The New Inquiry*, June 4, 2013, https://thenewinquiry.com/blog/the-primitive-accumulation-of-cool/.

Hoskyns, Barney. Review of *Yes New York/New York Noise/Post Punk 01*, by Various Artists. *Uncut*, 2003, *Rock's Backpages*.

"House of Rapture Lovers." *New Musical Express*, September 2, 2006.

Hughes, Walter. "In the Empire of the Beat: Discipline and Disco." *Electronica, Club and Dance Music*, 129–39. Edited by Mark J. Butler. London: Routledge, 2012.

Hulme, T. E. "Romanticism and Classicism." *Poetry Foundation*, https://www.poetryfoundation.org/articles/69477/romanticism-and-classicism.

Hynes, Dev. "The KKK Took My Baby Away." In *Punk Fiction: An Anthology of Short Stories Inspired by Punk*, 224–30. Edited by Janine Bullman. London: Portico, 2009.

Inscoe, Liam. "Burn the Dancefloor: The Raucous History of Dance Punk." *Sorry Scholar*, February 21, 2019, https://thesorryscholar.

com/2019/02/21/burn-the-dancefloor-the-raucus-history-of-dance-punk/.

James, Robin. "In but not of, of but not in: On\ Taste, Hipness, and White Embodiment." *Contemporary Aesthetics* 2 (2009). https://contempaesthetics.org/newvolume/pages/article.php?articleID=549.

Jameson, Fredric. *Postmodernism, or, the Cultural Logic of Late Capitalism*. Durham: Duke University Press, 1991.

Kapranos, Alex. *Sound Bites: Eating on Tour with Franz Ferdinand*. New York: Penguin, 2006.

King, Ian. *Appetite for Definition: An A-Z Guide to Rock Genres*. New York: Harper, 2018.

Kinzey, Jake. *The Sacred and the Profane: An Investigation of Hipsters*. Winchester: Zer0 Books, 2012.

Kronengold, Charles. "Exchange Theories in Disco, New Wave, and Album-Oriented Rock." *Criticism* 50, no. 1 (2008): 43–82.

Laing, Dave. *One Chord Wonders: Power and Meaning in Punk Rock*. Maidenhead: Open University Press, 1985.

Lawrence, Tim. *Love Saves the Day: A History of American Dance Music Culture, 1970–1979*. Durham: Duke University Press, 2003.

Lawrence, Tim. *Life and Death on the New York Dance Floor, 1980–1983*. Durham: Duke University Press, 2016.

"Leaders of the New School." *Muzik*, April 2003.

Leas, Ryan. *LCD Soundsystem's Sound of Silver*. New York: Bloomsbury, 2016.

Leland, John. *Hip: The History*. New York: Harper, 2004.

Lester, Paul. "ZE Records: 'It Was Like a Fairytale.'" *The Guardian*, July 30, 2009, https://www.theguardian.com/music/2009/jul/30/ze-records.

Lewitinn, Sarah, and Charles Aaron. "15 More to Watch: British Rock." *Spin*, February 2005.

Long, Pat. Review of *Pieces of the People We Love*, by The Rapture. *New Musical Express*, September 2, 2006.

Loss, Robert. *Nothing Has Been Done Before: Seeking the New in 21st-Century American Popular Music*. New York: Bloomsbury, 2017, https://doi.org/10.5040/9781501322051.ch-008.

Madden, David. "Cross-Dressing to Backbeats: The Status of the Electroclash Producer and the Politics of Electronic Music." *Dancecult* 4, no. 2 (2012): 27–47. https://dj.dancecult.net/index.php/dancecult/article/view/342/342.

Marcus, Greil. *Lipstick Traces: A Secret History of the Twentieth Century*. Cambridge, MA: Harvard University Press, 1989.

Marcus, Greil. *Ranters & Crowd Pleasers: Punk in Pop Music, 1977–92*. New York: Doubleday, 1993.

MasterClass. "Dance-Punk Music Guide: 5 Notable Dance-Punk Acts." https://www.masterclass.com/articles/dance-punk-music-guide.

Masud, Noreen. "A Horizon Line: Flat Style in Contemporary Women's Poetry." *Textual Practice* (2022), https://doi.org/10.1080/0950236X.2022.2030512.

Mattson, Kevin. *We're Not Here to Entertain: Punk Rock, Ronald Reagan, and the Real Culture War of 1980s America*. New York: Oxford University Press, 2020.

McDermott, Matt. "Rewind: The Rapture—House of Jealous Lovers." *Resident Advisor*, September 14, 2019, https://ra.co/reviews/24209.

McLeod, Kembrew, and Peter DiCola. *Creative License: The Law and Culture of Digital Sampling*. Durham: Duke University Press, 2011.

McWilliams, Douglas. *The Flat White Economy: How the Digital Economy Is Transforming London and Other Cities of the Future*. London: Duckworth Overlook, 2015.

Mikkonen, Kai. "Artificial Africa in the European Avant-Garde: Marinetti and Tzara." In *Europa! Europa? The Avant Garde, Modernism and the Fate of the Continent*, 391–407. Edited by Sascha Bru, Jan Baetens, Benedikt Hjartarson, Peter Nicholls, Tania Ørum, and Hubert van den Berg. Berlin: De Gruyter, 2009.

Mills, Fred. "Delta 5: Delta Force." *Harp*, March 2006, *Rock's Backpages*.

Moore, Allan F., and Remy Martin. *Rock: The Primary Text*. London: Routledge, 2018.

Moore, Ryan. *Sells Like Teen Spirit: Music Youth Culture and Social Crisis*. New York: New York University Press, 2010.

Morley, Paul. "Au Pairs: Every Home Should Have Four." *New Musical Express*, October 11, 1980. *Rock's Backpages*.

Moss, Jeremiah. *Vanishing New York: How a Great City Lost Its Soul*. New York: HarperCollins, 2017.

Murphy, James. "On Losing One's Edge." *Five Dials*, no. 13 (2009): 9.

Naylor, Todd. "Disco Punk Explosion!" *Muzik*, April 2003.

Naylor, Todd. "This Is New Rave." *New Musical Express*, June 17, 2006.

Needham, Alex. "Morrissey: 'Are you enjoying the hysteria?' Alex: 'Yeah, we're loving it.'" *New Musical Express*, May 22, 2004.

Neocleous, Mark. "Resisting Resilience." *Radical Philosophy* 178 (2013). https://www.radicalphilosophyarchive.com/issue-files/rp178_commentary_neocleous_resisting_resilience.pdf.

Ngai, Sianne. *Our Aesthetic Categories: Zany, Cute, Interesting*. Cambridge, MA: Harvard University Press, 2012.

Ngai, Sianne. "Stuplimity: Shock and Boredom in Twentieth-Century Aesthetics." *Postmodern Culture* 10, no. 2 (2000).

Ngai, Sianne. *Ugly Feelings*. Cambridge, MA: Harvard University Press, 2007.

O'Brien, Lucy. "Can I Have a Taste of Your Ice Cream?" *Punk & Post Punk* 1, no. 1 (2011): 27–40.

Okereke, Kele. "The Kick." *Five Dials*, no. 13 (2009): 21–3.

Okereke, Kele. "Shoplifting." In *Punk Fiction: An Anthology of Short Stories Inspired by Punk*, 32–8. Edited by Janine Bullman. London: Portico, 2009.

Olopade, Dayo. "The Hipster." In *Black Cool: One Thousand Streams of Blackness*, 39–45. Edited by Rebecca Walker. Berkeley: Soft Skull Press, 2012.

Partridge, Christopher. *Dub in Babylon: Understanding the Evolution and Significance of Dub Reggae in Jamaica and Britain from King Tubby to Post-Punk*. Sheffield: Equinox, 2010.

Pawson, John, and Lucy Orta. "To be minimalist … or maximalist?" *The Guardian*, April 19, 2004, https://www.theguardian.com/culture/2004/apr/19/guesteditors1.

Peterson, Richard A. "Understanding Audience Segmentation: From Elite and Mass to Omnivore and Univore." *Poetics* 21, no. 4 (1992): 243–58.

Petridis, Alex. "'This Is Going to Look Really Bad.'" *The Guardian*, October 7, 2005, https://www.theguardian.com/music/2005/oct/07/popandrock.blocparty.

Pierrot, Grégory. *Decolonize Hipsters*. New York: OR Books, 2021.

Pike, Gemma. "Bloc Party frontman Kele Okereke on Silent Alarm's Biggest Tracks." *The J Files*, May 14, 2020, https://www.abc.net.au/doublej/music-reads/features/bloc-party-silent-alarm-kele-okereke/12248212.

Platt, Alan. "No Chance." *SoHo Weekly News*, January 7, 1979.

Pountain, Dick, and David Robbins. *Cool Rules: Anatomy of an Attitude*. London: Reaktion, 2000.

Rambali, Paul. Review of *Entertainment!*, by Gang of Four. *New Musical Express*, October 6, 1979. *Rock's Backpages*.

Rambali, Paul. "Why is This Man Hip but a Complete Failure?: Michael Zilkha and ZE Records." *New Musical Express*, December 5, 1981, *Rock's Backpages*.

Raymer, Miles. "Control, Chaos, and the Fury of Bloc Party's 'Silent Alarm.'" *Riot Fest*, July 2, 2019, https://riotfest.org/2019/07/02/control-chaos-bloc-party/.

Rees, William David James. "Future Nostalgia? 21st Century Disco." *Dancecult* 13, no. 1 (2021): 36–53. https://dj.dancecult.net/index.php/dancecult/article/view/1195/1015.

Reynolds, Simon. Review of *They Threw Us All in a Trench and Stuck a Monument on Top*, by Liars. *Uncut*, September 2002, *Rock's Backpages*.

Reynolds, Simon. *Rip It Up and Start Again: Postpunk 1978–1984*. New York: Penguin, 2005.

Reynolds, Simon. *Totally Wired: Postpunk Interviews and Overviews*. Berkeley: Soft Skull, 2009.

Reynolds, Simon. *Retromania: Pop Culture's Addiction to Its Own Past*. New York: Faber and Faber, 2011.

Rodgers, Daniel. "WTF Is Indie Sleaze and Is It Actually Making a Comeback?" *Dazed*, October 29, 2021, https://www.dazeddigital.com/fashion/article/54603/1/wtf-is-indie-sleaze-comeback-tiktok-trend-y2k-chanel-saint-laurent-cobrasnake.

Rogers, Jude. Review of *Silent Alarm*, by Bloc Party. *The Word*, March 2005, *Rock's Backpages*.

Roholt, Tiger C. *Groove: A Phenomenology of Rhythmic Nuance*. New York: Bloomsbury, 2014.

Rosen, Jody. "The End of LCD Soundsystem: How a chubby 'old' guy became king of the hipsters." *Slate*, April 4, 2011, https://slate.com/culture/2011/04/lcd-soundsystem-how-a-chubby-old-guy-became-king-of-the-hipsters.html.

Ross, Tim. "Something Like a Phenomenon: The Complete 99 Records Story." *Tuba Frenzy*, no. 4 (Spring 1998).

Roth, Madeline. "Bloc Party's Kele Okereke on Their 'Cold' New Album: 'Everyone's F-cking Everyone Over.'" *The Daily Beast*, May 1, 2022, https://www.thedailybeast.com/bloc-partys-kele-okereke-on-the-ugly-fury-behind-alpha-games.

Rubin, Mike. "The 99 Records Story." *Red Bull Music Academy*, May 19, 2013, https://daily.redbullmusicacademy.com/2013/05/99-records-feature.

Rushkoff, Douglas. *Present Shock: When Everything Happens Now*. New York: Current, 2013.

"Sal Principato on Liquid Liquid's Optimo." *Ban Ban Ton Ton*, April 30, 2020, https://banbantonton.com/2020/04/30/sal-principato-on-liquid-liquids-optimo/.

Savage, Jon. Review of *Entertainment!*, by Gang of Four. *Melody Maker*, October 6, 1979. *Rock's Backpages*.

Savage, Jon. *England's Dreaming: Anarchy, Sex Pistols, Punk Rock and Beyond*. New York: St. Martin's, 2002.

Scheinbaum, John J. *Good Music: What It Is and Who Gets to Decide*. Chicago: University of Chicago Press, 2018.

Schreiber, Ryan. Review of *Echoes*, by The Rapture. *Pitchfork*, September 9, 2003, https://pitchfork.com/reviews/albums/6693-echoes/.

Shapiro, Peter. *Turn the Beat Around: The Secret History of Disco.* London: Faber, 2005.

Shelton, Emily. "Q and Not U's Recreation Myth." *WVAU*, October 26, 2017, http://wvau.org/3661/archives/q-and-not-us-recreation-myth/.

Silverton, Peter. "ZE Records." *New Sounds New Style*, July 1981, *Rock's Backpages*.

Sommer, Tim. "Liquid Liquid: The Most Important NY Band You've Never Heard Of." *The Observer*, July 16, 2015, https://observer.com/2015/07/liquid-liquid-the-most-important-ny-band-youve-never-heard-of/.

Southall, Nick. Review of *Silent Alarm*, by Bloc Party. *The Stylus*, February 14, 2005.

Spice, Anton. "Funk in Opposition: The Post-punk Dance Continuum from 1977 to the Present Day." *WaxPoetics*, October 6, 2021, https://www.waxpoetics.com/article/the-post-punk-dance-continuum-from-1977-to-the-present-day/.

Spitz, Marc. "Franz Ferdinand." *Spin*, November 2005.

Stein, Samuel. *Capital City: Gentrification and the Real Estate State.* London: Verso, 2019.

Steinhoff, Heike. "Hipster Culture: A Definition." In *Hipster Culture: Transnational and Intersectional Perspectives*, 1–24. Edited by Heike Steinhoff. New York: Bloomsbury, 2021.

Strauss, David. "Groove Is in the Art: An Interview with !!!'s Nic Offer." *Electronic Beats*, April 25, 2013, https://www.electronicbeats.net/an-interview-with-nic-offer/.

Stubbs, David. *Future Days: Krautrock and the Building of Modern Germany.* London: Faber & Faber, 2014.

Stubbs, David. "The Thin Boys: Post-Punk Funk." *Record Collector*,
    January 2, 2019, https://recordcollectormag.com/articles/
    post-punk-funk.

Sullivan, Jim. "Liquid Liquid, V: Streets, Boston MA." *The Boston
    Globe*, December 4, 1981, *Rock's Backpages*.

Sutcliffe, Phil. "The Delta of Venus: Delta 5." *Sounds*, August 2,
    1980, *Rock's Backpages*.

Sylvester, Nick. Review of *DFA Records Presents: Compilation #1*,
    by DFA Records. *Pitchfork*, December 9, 2003, https://
    pitchfork.com/reviews/albums/2031-dfa-records-presents-
    compilation-1/.

"Syncopation in pop/rock music." *Open Music Theory*, http://
    openmusictheory.com/syncopation.html.

Tortorici, Dayna. "You Know It When You See It." In *What Was
    the Hipster? A Sociological Investigation*, 122–135. Edited by
    Mark, Greif, Kathleen Ross, and Dayna Tortorici. New York: n+1
    Foundation, 2010.

Van Meter, William. "LCD Soundsystem." *Spin*, February 2005.

Veal, Michael. *Dub: Soundscapes and Shattered Songs in Jamaican
    Reggae*. Middletown: Wesleyean University Press, 2013.

Ware, Tony. "The Rapture's Luke Jenner on Living in San Francisco,
    Being the 'Black Sheep' of Sub Pop, and Learning to Be
    Positive." *SF Weekly*, October 7, 2011, https://archives.sfweekly.
    com/shookdown/2011/10/07/the-raptures-luke-jenner-on-
    living-in-san-francisco-being-the-black-sheep-of-sub-pop-
    and-learning-to-be-positive.

Wijesooriya, Ruvan. *LCD*. Brooklyn: powerHouse Books, 2021.

Wilkinson, David. *Post-Punk, Politics and Pleasure in Britain*. London:
    Palgrave Macmillan, 2016.

Wilson, Anna. "The Legendary Liquid Liquid— Interview, Part 1." *Clash*, August 6, 2010, https://www.clashmusic.com/features/the-legendary-liquid-liquid-interview-part-1.

Wilson, Anna. "The Legendary Liquid Liquid— Interview, Part 2." *Clash*, August 6, 2010, https://www.clashmusic.com/features/the-legendary-liquid-liquid-interview-part-2.

Wilson, Carl. "A Guide to Music Jargon." *The Globe and Mail*, January 8, 2005.

Wilson, Scott, Chal Ravens, April Clare Welsh, and Tam Gunn. "What the hell was blog house? 30 classic tracks from a great lost era." *FACT Magazine*, June 16, 2016, https://www.factmag.com/2016/06/16/30-best-blog-house-tracks/.

Winnubst, Shannon. *Way Too Cool: Selling Out Race and Ethics*. New York: Columbia University Press, 2015.

Wodtke, Larissa. "The Irony and the Ecstasy: The Queer Aging of Pet Shop Boys and LCD Soundsystem in Electronic Dance Music." *Dancecult* 11, no. 1 (2019): 30–52. https://doi.org/10.12801/1947-5403.2019.11.01.03.

Wodtke, Larissa. "MP3 as Contentious Message: When Infinite Repetition Fuses with the Acoustic Sphere." In *Seriality and Texts for Young People: The Compulsion to Repeat*, 237–57. Edited by Mavis Reimer, Nyala Ali, Deanna England, and Melanie Dennis Unrau. London: Palgrave Macmillan, 2014.

Young, Rob. "Liquid Ecstasy: LCD Soundsystem: *LCD Soundsystem*." *Uncut*, February 2005, *Rock's Backpages*.

Zukin, Sharon. *Naked City: The Death and Life of Authentic Urban Places*. New York: Oxford University Press, 2009.